Doublespeak
DEFINED

Also by William Lutz

Doublespeak

The New Doublespeak

Doublespeak
Doublespeak
Doublespeak
Doublespeak

Doublespeak

DEFINED

CUT THROUGH THE BULL****
AND GET THE POINT

William Lutz

William Lutz (signature)

HarperResource
A Division of HarperCollinsPublishers

Nov. 4, 2000

HarperCollins books may be purchased for educational, business, or sales promotional use. For information please write: Special Markets Department, HarperCollins Publishers, Inc., 10 East 53rd Street, New York, NY 10022.

FIRST EDITION

Designed by Kim Llewellyn

Library of Congress Cataloging-in-Publication Data
Lutz, William.
    Doublespeak defined : cut through the bull**** and get the point.
William Lutz. — 1st ed.
      p. cm.
    Includes index.
    ISBN 0-06-273412-1
    1. Jargon (Terminology). English language—Jargon. I. Title.
P409.L87   1999
427—dc21   99-19253
                                       CIP

99 00 01 02 03 ❖/RRD 10 9 8 7 6 5 4 3 2 1

For my son, Bill

Contents

Introduction

The great enemy of clear language is insincerity. When there is a gap between one's real and one's declared aims, one turns as it were instinctively to long words and exhausted idioms, like a cuttlefish squirting out ink.

GEORGE ORWELL,
"Politics and the English Language" 1946

For George Orwell, language was an instrument for "expressing and not for concealing or preventing thought." In his most biting comment in his essay, Orwell observes that "In our time, political speech and writing are largely the defense of the indefensible. . . . Political language has to consist largely of euphemism, question-begging and sheer cloudy vagueness. . . . Political language . . . is designed to make lies sound truthful and murder respectable, and to give an appearance of solidity to pure wind."

Today, used cars are no longer "pre-owned" but "experienced cars," and black-and-white television sets come with "non-multicolor capability." Pot holes have been transformed into "pavement deficiencies." We don't have new taxes, just some "revenue enhancement" through new "user fees." And those people wandering our city streets are "non-goal oriented members of society," while poor people are better known as "fiscal underachievers." Crime is decreasing, partly because what was once a robbery of an automatic teller machine has become an "unauthorized withdrawal." Airplanes don't crash, they just have "uncontrolled contact with the ground." The U.S. Army doesn't kill the enemy anymore, it "services the target," like any service industry.

Doublespeak is not a matter of subjects and verbs agreeing; it's a matter of words and facts agreeing. Basic to doublespeak is incongruity, the incongruity between what is said, or left unsaid, and what really is. It's the incongruity between the word and the referent, between seem and be, between the essential function of language (communication) and what doublespeak does (mislead, distort, deceive, inflate, circumvent, obfuscate). Doublespeak turns lies told by politicians into "being economical with the truth," sewage sludge into "regulated organic nutrients" that do not stink but "exceed the odor threshold," the death of a patient in a hospital into "negative patient care outcome," an explosion and fire in a nuclear power plant into an "energetic disassembly" and "rapid oxidation."

Everywhere we turn we encounter the language with which Orwell was so concerned. It's not an economic recession but a "period of accelerated negative growth" or simply "negative economic growth." There's no such thing as acid rain; according to the Environmental Protection Agency it's "poorly buffered precipitation," or more impressively, "atmospheric deposition of anthropogenetically-derived acidic substances," or more subtly, "wet deposition." And those aren't gangsters, mobsters, the Mafia, or La Cosa Nostra in Atlantic City; according to the "New Jersey Division of Gaming Enforcement" (a doublespeak title which avoids the use of that dreaded word "gambling") they're "members of a career-offender cartel."

Doublespeak has become so common in everyday living that we no longer pay any attention to it. Indeed, we seem to take it for granted, as if such language is the normal way of communicating, or more correctly, not communicating. Even worse, when we do notice it, we don't react. We don't protest when we're asked to check our packages at the desk "for your convenience" when it's not for our convenience at all but for someone else's convenience. We see advertisements for "deep-chilled chickens," "virgin vinyl," or "synthetic glass," but we don't question the language or the supposed quality of the product. We don't challenge the politicians who speak not of slums or ghettos but of the "inner city" or "substandard housing" where the "disadvantaged" live, thus avoiding any mention of the poor who have to live in filthy, poorly heated, ramshackle apartments or houses.

Doublespeak that calls a bribe a "rebate" or "after sales service," the illegal overthrow of a legitimate government "destabilizing a government," and lies "strategic misrepresentations" is language that avoids responsibility, that makes the bad seem good, the negative appear positive, something unpleasant appear attractive, language that only appears to communicate. It's language designed to alter our perception of reality and corrupt our thinking. Ultimately, doublespeak breeds suspicion, cynicism, distrust and, hostility.

Doublespeak strikes at the function of language—communication between people and social groups—with serious and far-reaching consequences. Our political system depends upon an informed electorate to make decisions in selecting candidates for office and deciding issues of public policy. As doublespeak becomes the coin of the political realm, as doublespeak drives out a language of public discourse that really communicates, speakers and listeners become convinced that they understand such language. We speak today of politicians who don't lie but "misspeak," of "dysfunction behavior" not murder, of a "predawn vertical insertion" not the invasion of another country, of "violence processing" or the "use of force" not of war. When we use such language believing that we are using the public discourse necessary for the health and well being of our community, then, I believe, the world of *1984* is upon us.

To the Reader

In an age of political correctness and hypersensitivity, not to mention rampant corporate and government linguistic fraud and deception, you need all the help you can get. You need to be on constant alert so that those who create and use doublespeak can't use it to control, manipulate, deceive, use, and abuse you. Think of this book as a survival manual for the contemporary linguistic jungle. All of the doublespeak in this book is real; none of it is made up. I have carefully recorded the source and context for each example. All of it has been used by someone to get away with something. Do you know what General Motors meant when it announced a "volume-related production schedule adjustment," or what the hospital meant when it said the patient died as a result of a "diagnostic misadventure of a high magnitude"? Well, that's what this book is for: to help you wade through the flood of doublespeak that is engulfing our society, to wade through the sewage that passes for communication these days.

I have written this book to assure you that there is nothing wrong with you or any of the millions of other perfectly sane, intelligent Americans who wonder every day if the language they hear so often is a new foreign language, who wonder if there is something wrong with them because they don't understand what those politicians, bureaucrats, spin doctors, advertisers, and corporate hacks are saying. I do not pretend to have written a comprehensive manual of doublespeak. What you have in your hands is a brief guide that covers the most essential and egregious terms. For more complete coverage of doublespeak, I refer you to my previous books: *Doublespeak: From Revenue Enhancement to Terminal Living* (HarperCollins) and *The New Doublespeak: Why No One Knows What Anyone's Saying Anymore* (HarperCollins), and *The Cambridge Thesaurus of American English* (Cambridge University Press).

I would like to thank Susan Muaadi and Laurie Baker who gave of their time, skill, and intelligence in preparing this book for publication. I came to depend upon them, and especially Ms. Muaadi, for their consistency, sharp eye, and good humor. Theirs was an effort above and beyond the requirements of the job, an effort they gave cheerfully. For all that they contributed to this book I am deeply grateful.

Abbreviations

CIA	Central Intelligence Agency
DOI	Department of the Interior
DOD	Department of Defense
Doublespeak	*Doublespeak: From Revenue Enhancement to Terminal Living,* William Lutz (HarperCollins, 1989)
EPA	Environmental Protection Agency
FAA	Federal Aviation Administration
FBI	Federal Bureau of Investigation
NASA	National Aeronautics and Space Administration
New Doublespeak	*The New Doublespeak: Why No One Knows What Anyone's Saying Anymore,* William Lutz (HarperCollins, 1996)
NRC	Nuclear Regulatory Commission
PBS	Public Broadcasting System
USDA	United States Department of Agriculture

1

Transportation

....

accident *n.*
1. *abnormal occurrence* (NRC)
2. *event* (NRC)
3. *unusual event* (NRC)
4. *safety-related occurrence* (NRC)
5. *normally occurring abnormal occurrence* (NRC)
6. *reportable occurrences* (NRC)
7. *unintentional injury*
8. *an interaction with a car* or *a truck*
9. *anomaly* (NASA)

> • When the Challenger blew up, it wasn't an accident;
> according to NASA, it was an "anomaly."
> —*Orlando* (FL) *Sentinel,* Mar. 2, 1986

10. *anthropogenically induced event*
11. *fortuitous event*

air bag *n.*
1. *supplemental inflatable restraint system*
2. *non-belt automatic restraint system*
        see *seat belt*

airline flight delay *n.*
schedule irregularity

auto mechanic *n.*
automotive internist; see also *car mechanic*

automobile accident *n.*
1. *vehicular malscrusion*
2. *vehicular interaction*

breakdown (OF AN AIRPLANE) *n.*
change of equipment

breakdown (OF AN AUTOMOBILE) *v.*
1. *fail to proceed*

> ● Rolls [Royce] officials still do not say the product
> breaks down, but rather "fails to proceed."
> —*Time,* Sept. 2, 1985

2. *go technical*
3. *suffer a malfunction*

bus *n.*
customer conveyance mobile lounge

> ● A flight attendant announced that passengers would
> be taken from the departure gate to their plane by a
> "customer conveyance mobile lounge," also known as
> a bus.   —*Quarterly Review of Doublespeak,* Apr. 1988

bus driver *n.*
1. *transit coach operator*

> ● The City of Simi Valley, California, is looking for a

"Transit Coach Operator." In other words, they want to hire a bus driver.

—*Quarterly Review of Doublespeak,* July 1988

see also *cab driver*

2. *certified adolescent transportation specialist*

    ● A Minnesota school bus company calls its drivers "certified adolescent transportation specialists."

—*Reader's Digest,* Jan. 1988

cab driver *n.*
urban transportation specialist

car engine *n.*
power module

car mechanic *n.*
1. *automotive internist*
2. *auto installation specialist*
   see also *auto mechanic*

car salesperson *n.*
1. *transportation counselor*

    ● People who sell cars are sometimes referred to as "transportation counselors." —*The New Doublespeak*
   see also *used car*

2. *product consultant*
3. *purchase advisor of previously distinguished automobiles*
4. *new car accountant*

car wash *n.*
vehicle appearance specialists

• The residents of Vancouver no longer have to settle for a mere car wash for their automobiles; now they can go to Esprit Auto Detailing, the "vehicle appearance specialists."

—*Quarterly Review of Doublespeak,* Oct. 1987

chauffeur *n.*
aides who drive

• Members of the governor's staff do not have chauffeurs. They have "aides who drive."

—*Philadelphia Inquirer,* July 15, 1982

crash (AIRPLANE) *n.*

1. *uncontrolled contact with the ground* (FAA)
2. *unscheduled contact with the ground* (FAA)
3. *failure to maintain clearance from the ground* (FAA)

• The National Transportation Safety Board cited the following as the probable causes of a helicopter crash that killed three people: "flying into bad weather and failure to maintain clearance from the ground."

—*Associated Press,* Nov. 14, 1987

4. *controlled flight into terrain* or *CFIT* (FAA)
5. *involuntary conversion of a 727*
6. *hard landing*

• When six Marines were killed and eleven injured in a helicopter crash during training, officials called the incident a "hard landing."

—*Seattle* (WA) *Press-Inquirer,* Nov. 21, 1984

crash dummy *n.*
instrumented anthropomorphic device

driveway *n.*
auto reception area

emergency vehicle *n.*
major incident response unit

garage *n.*
motor room

holes (IN AN AIRPLANE WING) *n.*
surface irregularities

> • Eastern Airlines officials did not find holes in two of
> the airplanes they inspected; they found "surface
> irregularities."
>
> —*Spy,* June 1989

jeep *n.*
high mobility multipurpose wheeled vehicle (DOD)

life preserver *n.*
1. *water device*
2. *personal preservation flotation device* (DOD)

> • The U.S. Coast Guard decided on rules changes
> designed to make life jackets more familiar to the
> average recreational boater. Instead of referring to
> "personal floatation devices" (or PFDs), the new regu-
> lations will now refer to such things as an "off-shore
> life jacket," a "near-shore buoyant vest," and a
> "throwable device."
>
> —*Bridgeport* (CT) *Telegram,* Dec. 6, 1989

lost luggage *n.*
misconnect rate

> • Airlines don't worry about how many bags they lose; they worry about the "misconnect rate."
> —*New York Times*, Jan. 19, 1990

mud flap *n.*
splash and spray suppression device

> • A bill in Congress does not refer to mud flaps on trucks but to "splash and spray suppression devices."
> —*Philadelphia Inquirer*, Mar. 17, 1987

pothole *n.*
pavement deficiency

> • In Tucson, Arizona, there are no potholes, but there are some "pavement deficiencies."
> —*Things No One Ever Tells You*, Warner Books, 1980

seat belt *n.*
automatic restraint

> • The National Highway Traffic Safety Administration announced its decision on the use of seat belts and air bags in automobiles...that companies can comply with the regulation by equipping new vehicles with a "non-belt automatic restraint system" for the driver and a "dynamically-tested manual lap-shoulder belt for the right front passenger."
> —*Federal Register*, Mar. 30, 1987

see also *airbag*

sidewalk *n.*
pedestrian facility

space suit *n.*
extravehicular mobility unit

> • You may call them space suits, but at Hamilton Standard, which makes them, they call them "Extravehicular Mobility Units," or EMUs.
> —*Quarterly Review of Doublespeak,* Jan. 1989

speed bumps *n.*
undulated road

traffic signal *n.*
1. *transitron*
2. *electronically adjusted, color-coded, vehicular flow control mechanism*

used car *n.*
1. *previously distinguished automobile*

> • "Pre-owned" and "experienced" are no longer the preferred doublespeak terms for used cars. Now they're "previously distinguished" cars.
> —*Quarterly Review of Doublespeak,* Oct. 1988

2. *experienced car*
3. *pre-driven*
4. *pre-owned*
   see also *car salesperson*

windshield wiper *n.*
adverse weather visibility device

> • You and I call it a windshield wiper, but . . . the federal requirement calls for an "adverse weather visibility device." —*Quarterly Review of Doublespeak,* July 1988

wrecked car *n.*

victim of major impact

> • Cars brought to Aston Martin for repairs after an accident are never called "wrecks." They're called "victims of major impacts."

> —*Wall Street Journal,* Mar. 25, 1993

2

Science
and Nature

....

acid rain *n.*
1. *poorly buffered precipitation* (EPA)
2. *atmospheric deposition of anthropogenically-derived acidic
substances* (EPA)

> ● "Atmospheric deposition of anthropogenically-derived
> acidic substances" is destroying the ecosystem.
> —*New York Times*, Mar. 1, 1984

3. *wet deposition* (EPA)

> ● The Environmental Protection Agency promoted the
> use of the term "wet deposition" instead of acid rain.
> —*The New Doublespeak*

4. *transit particle deposition from an unidentifiable source*
(EPA)

> ● The latest term for acid rain is "transit particle depo-
> sition from an unidentifiable source."
> —*Quarterly Review of Doublespeak*, July 1988

acorn *n.*
a nut partially enclosed by a cupule of bracts

> ● A scientist writes about a tree that is "characterized within the family Fagaceae . . . by a nut partially enclosed by a cupule of bracts." That's an oak tree with acorns. —*New York Times*, Mar. 1, 1984

artificial flavor *n.*
natural flavor

burning of trash *n.*
1. *thermotreatment of waste*
2. *thermomatically treated waste*

cast iron *n.*
ferrous-carbon alloy

cave. *n.*
erosional feature

change something *v.*
effect a transformation

child *n.*
ambulatory biped

disposable *mod.*
single use

> ● Kodak does not sell a disposable camera, an unacceptable term in an age of environmental awareness. Kodak sells instead a "single use" camera.

Terms such as "recyclable," "degradable," and "environmentally friendly" have no fixed meaning. When Glad brought out a plastic trash bag it called "biodegradable," Mobil Oil, the maker of Hefty trash bags, maintained that the plastic trash bag is impervious to degradation. But the sales of Glad trash bags went up while those of Hefty went down. So Mobil brought out its own "photodegradable" trash bag. This doublespeak attracted the attention of the attorneys general of seven states who filed a lawsuit against Mobil for claiming that its Hefty trash bags have a "special ingredient that promotes their breakdown after exposure to elements like sun, wind and rain." The Hefty boxes carried the claim that once nature has "triggered" their new additive "these bags will continue to break down into harmless particles even after they are buried in a landfill." Meanwhile, Mobil admitted that in its own tests conducted in 1988 it took 30 days in the blazing sun of the Arizona desert for a bag to reach a satisfactory level of decomposition, and then it simply broke open and dumped its contents on the ground. In other less sunny climates it takes about 120 days for the bag to break down, and in a sunless landfill it won't break down at all. Mike Levy, Mobil's lobbyist, was quoted as saying: "We're talking out of both sides of our mouth. Degradability is just a marketing tool." Mobil did stop using the word "photodegradable" for its Hefty trash bags because of the lawsuit filed by the attorneys general.

—*Advertising Age,* Nov. 13, 1989; *New York Times,* Feb. 17, 1990; Jan. 8, 1991; *Liberal Opinion Week,* June 25, 1990

dump *n.*

1. *public waste reception center*
2. *reutilization marketing yard*

- You may call it a junkyard, but to the federal government it's a "reutilization marketing yard."

—*Federal Register*

3. *resource development park*

> • To some, it's a dump; to others, however, it's a "resource development park." —*The New Doublespeak*

4. *landfill*
5. *volume reduction plant*

> • New Canaan, Connecticut, which is the community with the highest per-capita income in New England, does not have a dump; it has a "volume reduction plant." —*Fairpress,* May 19, 1988

dumping waste (IN AN OCEAN) *n.*
deep ocean placement

dumping waste (IN A RIVER) *n.*
organic loading

> • What do you call dumping 22,000 pounds of organic chemical waste into the Mississippi River every day? You call it "organic loading."
> —*Smithsonian,* Feb. 1993

dust *n.*
airborne particles

earthquake *n.*
seismic event

explosion *n.*
energetic disassembly

fake beef *n.*
1. *restructured beef*
2. *textured meat alternative*

fake cheese *n.*
cheese analog

fake crab meat *n.*
surimi-based crab analog

fake diamonds *n.*
real counterfeit diamonds

fake jewels *n.*
faux jewels

fake leather *n.*
genuine imitation leather

fake meat *n.*
restructured muscle product

fence *n.*
neoecological boundary

fire *n.*
1. *incendiary event*

> • A nuclear power plant calls a fire an "incendiary event." *—Quarterly Review of Doublespeak,* Apr. 1988

2. *rapid oxidation*
3. *oxidation event*

garbage *n.*
post-consumer secondary materials

glass *n.*
fused silicate

glue *n.*
cold adhesive bond

ground bone *n.*
1. *mechanically separated meat*
2. *calcium*

heat *v.*
rethermalize

heat pollution *n.*
thermal enrichment

human-made *mod.*
anthropogenic

hunt *v.*
1. *harvest*

> • The state of Florida preferred the word "harvest" to the word "hunt" when it allowed hunters to kill 3,500 alligators.
> —*Quarterly Review of Doublespeak,* Jan. 1989

2. *renaturalize*

kill (ANIMALS) *v.*
1. *harvest;* see also *hunt*
2. *manage wildlife*
3. *depopulate*

Non Sequitur

© 1998 Washington Post Writers Group. Reprinted with permission.

light switch *n.*
ideogram illumination intensity adjustment potentiometer

mousetrap *n.*
rodent elimination device

natural *mod.*
biogenic

nuclear waste *n.*
1. *valuable, important nuclear materials*
2. *monitored retrievable storage*

> • Nuclear waste has been called "valuable, important nuclear materials" and nuclear waste dumps referred to as "monitored retrievable storage."
>
> *—The New Doublespeak*

oil spill *n.*
tanker accident

> ● The Interior Department will no longer use the phrase "oil spill"; from now on it will refer to "tanker accidents." —*U.S. News and World Report*, July 10, 1989

open pit for burning trash *n.*
air curtain incinerator

> ● Air curtain incineration occurs in an air curtain incinerator, which means burning trash in an open pit. —*Solid Waste Report*, Jan. 28, 1993

plastic *n.*
synthetic glass

plastic trash bag *n.*
waste management bag

> ● Kmart sells "waste management bags" not plastic trash bags. —*Quarterly Review of Doublespeak*, Apr. 1991

plow *n.*
earth-engaging equipment

polluted *mod.*
environmentally stabilized

> ● While residents complained of polluted beaches and virtually nonexistent clean-up, Exxon executives referred to the beaches in Alaska affected by the *Valdez* oil spill as "environmentally stabilized." —*The New Doublespeak*

rotten fruits and vegetables *n.*
distressed produce

sewage plant *n.*
wastewater conveyance facility

sewage sludge *n.*
1. *regulated organic nutrients*
2. *bioslurp*
3. *organic biomass*

> • Some people may call the residue of treated sewage "sludge," but to John Gonzales of the Reno-Sparks, Nevada, sewage treatment plant it's "organic biomass."
> —*Quarterly Review of Doublespeak,* Apr. 1990

4. *biosolids*

> It might look like sludge to you, but others call it "biosolids."   —*The New Doublespeak*

5. *regulated wastewater residuals*

sewer *n.*
wastewater conveyance facility

sugar *n.*
crystallized, evaporated cane juice

sunk *mod.*
comfortably settled at the bottom

> • Workers tried for two days to move a replica of the 17th-century ship *Godspeed* into the water. Now only the masts and rear deck are visible in the harbor. "We don't consider it sunk," a spokesperson said. "We consider it comfortably settled on the bottom of the river."
>
> —*Philadelphia Inquirer,* Sept. 16, 1984

thermometer *n.*
digital fever computer

trash incinerator *n.*
1. *resource recovery facility*
2. *thermal processing unit*
3. *thermal soil remediation unit*

vinyl *n.*
vegetarian leather

> • Drew Bernstein, the Los Angeles clothes designer, sells dresses made of "vegetarian leather."
>
> —*Philadelphia Inquirer,* Jan. 14, 1990

wastepaper basket *n.*
user-friendly, space-effective, flexible deskside sortation unit

> • Government officials in Toronto, Canada, paid $123.80 [Canadian] each for "user friendly, space effective, flexible deskside sortation units," more commonly known as wastepaper baskets.
>
> —*Toronto Sun,* May 13, 1992

wave *n.*
sea-air interface climatic disturbance

wood *n.*
three-dimensional biopolymer composites

wood pulp *n.*
1. *alpha cellulose*
2. *powdered cellulose*
3. *source of fiber*

zoo *n.*
wildlife conservation program with some permanent facilities

> • The Vancouver park board received a proposal for a new "Stanley Park interpretation and wildlife plan" to replace the Stanley Park Zoo. "I don't see it as a zoo," said the head of the park board. She prefers to call it a "wildlife conservation program with some permanent facilities." —*Vancouver Sun,* May 15, 1993

3

War and the Military

....

ambush *n.*
pro-active counterattack (DOD)

ambush *v.*
1. *engage the enemy on all sides* (DOD)
2. *meeting engagement*

antipersonnel bomb *n.*
area denial weapon (DOD)

> • "Area denial weapons" are cluster bombs, previously known as antipersonnel bombs.
> —*The New Doublespeak*

antisatellite weapon *n.*
kinetic kill vehicle (DOD)

atomic bomb *n.*
1. *nuclear warhead*
2. *strategic weapon*
3. *tactical weapon*

4. *nuclear device*
5. *device that is exploding*
6. *re-entry system*
7. *physics package* (DOD)

> • During congressional hearings on the Intermediate-range Nuclear Forces treaty, Secretary of Defense Frank Carlucci kept using the phrase "physics package," which meant the atomic warhead on intermediate-range missiles.
> —*Quarterly Review of Doublespeak*, Jan. 1989

atomic explosion *n.*
nuclear event

atomic war *n.*
thermonuclear or *nuclear exchange*

attack *n.*
assuming an offensive posture

> • The military refers to attack as "assuming an offensive posture."
> —*Quarterly Review of Doublespeak*, Apr. 1988

bayonet *n.*
weapons system

bomb *v.*
1. *effective delivery of ordnance* (DOD)

> • Phrases such as "effective delivery of ordnance" are not likely to invoke mental pictures of thousands of tons of bombs falling on buildings and people.
> —*The New Doublespeak*

Military doublespeak starts at the top with the name of the Department of Defense. America had a Department of War until 1947, when the military pulled off the doublespeak coup of the century. On July 27, 1947, President Harry S. Truman signed the National Security Act of 1947, a law that completely reorganized the armed forces of the United States. Title II of that law carries the heading "Establishment of the National Military Establishment," and under Section 202 the post of Secretary of Defense is established. But it is in Section 205(a) that the real doublespeak is institutionalized: "The Department of War shall hereafter be designated the Department of the Army, and the title of the Secretary of War shall be changed to Secretary of the Army." Suddenly, war became "defense" with the Secretary of Defense in charge of the Department of Defense, which includes the Army, Navy, and Air Force.

Those who are willing to accept "defense" instead of "war" in the title of this government agency will perhaps agree to a few other changes in order to be consistent. The unpleasantness of 1914–1918 and 1939–1945 will be called World Defense I and World Defense II, Tolstoy's great novel will become *Defense and Peace,* and General William Tecumseh Sherman's comment will be changed to "Defense is Hell."

2. *visit the site* (DOD)
3. *degrade* (DOD)
4. *eliminate* (DOD)
5. *suppress* (DOD)
6. *neutralize* (DOD)
7. *take out* (DOD)
8. *sanitize the area* (DOD)
9. *cleanse* (DOD)
10. *conduct coercive diplomacy* (DOD)

11. *erode the will of the population* (DOD)
12. *prosecute the target* (DOD)
13. *terrain alteration* (DOD)
14. *disrupt*

> • Weapons systems don't drop bombs; they "visit a site" and "degrade," "neutralize," "attrit," "suppress," "eliminate," "cleanse," "sanitize," "impact," "decapitate" or "take out" their targets.   —*The New Doublespeak*

bomber (AIRCRAFT) *n.*
force package

> • "Force packages" or "weapons systems" visit sites— or planes drop bombs.   —*The New Doublespeak*

bombing *n.*
1. *protective reaction strike* (DOD)
2. *air support* (DOD)
3. *limited duration protective reaction strike* (DOD)
4. *coercive diplomacy* (DOD)
5. *armed reconnaissance* (DOD)

> • "Bombing raids" are a thing of the past; now, there are "armed reconnaissance" missions.
> —*Dictionary of Euphemism and Other Doublespeak*

6. *effective delivery of ordnance* (DOD)

> • "In Vietnam, American war planes conducted 'limited duration protective reaction strikes' during which they achieved an 'effective delivery of ordnance.'"
> —*The New Doublespeak*

7. *limited air interdiction* (DOD)

"Anti-personnel land mines pose no threat to people, Colonel. Only to personnel."

bomb load *n.*
payload

bullet wound *n.*
ballistically induced aperture in the subcutaneous environment

civilian casualties *n.*
collateral damage

> • When General Bernard Rogers was asked if collateral damage meant civilian casualties, he said "Yes."
> —*New York Times*, May 4, 1985

cockpit *n.*
missionized crew station

> • Once upon a time Air Force fighters had cockpits, but now they have "Missionized Crew Stations."
> —*USAF Fighter Weapons Review*, Summer 1988

combat *n.*
violence processing (DOD)

crash (MISSILE) *n.*
1. *early termination*

> • According to the First Strategic Aerospace Division at Vandenberg Air Force Base, "An anomaly occurred during the flight, which caused the early termination."
> —*New York Times*, Aug. 29, 1986

2. *prematurely terminated flight*

crash (MISSILE) *v.*
1. *cease to fly*

> • A U.S. military spokesman said the Cruise missile had "ceased to fly." —*New York Times*, Feb. 1, 1985

2. *impact with the ground prematurely*

3. *terminate five minutes earlier than planned*

> • A Canadian Forces spokesman said the missile had "terminated five minutes earlier than planned."
> —*Toronto Star,* Jan. 25, 1986

dead enemy soldiers *n.*
decommissioned aggressor quantum

dead soldier *n.*
non-viable asset

During the war in the Persian Gulf, massive bombing attacks became "efforts." Thousands of "weapons systems" or "force packages" "visited a site." These "weapons systems" "hit" "hard" and "soft targets." During their "visits," these "weapons systems" "degraded," "neutralized," "attrited," "suppressed," "eliminated," "cleansed," "sanitized," "impacted," "decapitated" or "took out" targets. A "healthy day of bombing" was achieved when more enemy "assets" were destroyed than expected.

If the "weapons systems" didn't achieve "effective results" during their first "visit," a "damage assessment study" determined whether the "weapons systems" would "revisit the site." Women, children or other civilians killed or wounded during these "visits," and any schools, hospitals, museums, houses or other "non-military" targets that were blown up, were "collateral damage," which is the undesired damage or casualties produced by the effects from "incontinent ordnance" or "accidental delivery of ordnance equipment."

destroy *v.*
suppress the target

discriminate *v.*
exclude

> • "We don't necessarily discriminate. We simply exclude certain types of people," said an ROTC instructor at the Massachusetts Institute of Technology on the military's ban on gays. —*Newsweek,* May 25, 1992

explosion *n.*
unplanned rapid ignition of solid fuel

> • The Pershing II missile did not explode; it was an "unplanned rapid ignition of solid fuel," said the U.S. Army spokesperson. —*Newsweek,* Jan. 21, 1985

failed *mod.*
sub-optimal

female soldiers *n.*
males with female features

> • During the war in the Persian Gulf, the Saudi government rejected the idea of female soldiers coming to their defense (women make up one-tenth of the U.S. forces), so it designated the women soldiers "males with female features." —*Time,* Feb. 25, 1991

flashlight *n.*
emergency exit light (DOD)

furniture *n.*
habitability improvements (U.S. Navy)

> • The U.S. Navy paid $31,672 for a couch, 20 dining room chairs, and a loveseat for the destroyer USS *Kidd*. The furniture was called "habitability improvements."
> —*Chicago Tribune Magazine,* Jan. 1, 1984

genocide *n.*
1. *ethnic cleansing*

> • When Serbian gunmen go door-to-door in a Bosnian town pulling Slavs and Roman Catholic Croats from their homes at gunpoint and herding them forcibly onto cattle trucks and deporting or later shooting them, the Serbs call it "ethnic cleansing."
> —*New York Times,* May 22, 1992

2. *depopulation*
3. *elimination of unreliable elements*

guest *n.*
customer

hammer *n.*
1. *interfibrous friction fastener*

> • In the Army, a hammer is an "interfibrous friction fastener."
> —*Quarterly Review of Doublespeak,* Apr. 1988

2. *multidirectional impact generator*

hostage *n.*
foreign guest

human being *n.*
soft target

- Bombs don't hit human beings; they hit "soft targets."

ICBM *n.*
1. *very large, potentially disruptive re-entry system*

- Colonel Frank Horton described the Titan II missile as "a very large, potentially disruptive re-entry system."
  —*Grand Forks* (ND) *Herald,* Mar. 13, 1983

2. *peacemaker*

- President Reagan named the MX missile the Peacemaker. —*New York Times Magazine,* May 26, 1985

invade *v.*
1. *execute preplanned missions*
2. *deploy troops*

Also during the Gulf War, the U.S. Army claimed that the Patriot missile "intercepted" 45 of 47 Scud missiles, but later the Army said the Patriot missile intercepted between 40% and 70% of the Scuds. President Bush claimed that Patriot missiles had killed 41 of 42 Scud warheads they had targeted. In testimony before a Congressional committee, Brigadier General Robert Drolet was asked to explain if President Bush was correct. Gen. Drolet said the claim was still correct because President Bush "did not say 'killed' or 'destroyed.'" What he said was "intercepted." And what does the Army mean by "intercept"? Replied Gen. Drolet, "A Patriot and Scud passed in the sky."

—*New York Times,* April 9, 1992;
Science, April 17, 1992

invasion *n.*

1. *predawn vertical insertion*

> ● White House officials called the invasion of Grenada a "predawn vertical insertion."
>
> —*New York Times,* Oct. 28, 1983

2. *incursion*
3. *preemptive counterattack* or *offensive*
4. *rescue mission*
5. *reconnaissance in force*
6. *deployment*
7. *aggressive defense*

> ● In the U.S. military, an aggressive offensive attack is also sometimes called an aggressive defense.
>
> —*Doublespeak*

8. *use of force*

> ● Senator Christopher Dodd was "not enthusiastic about the option of the use of force" proposed by the Clinton Administration in dealing with Haiti.
>
> —*New York Times,* Sept. 15, 1994

kill (HUMANS) *v.*

1. *unlawful* or *arbitrary deprivation of life* (U.S. Department of State)
2. *neutralize the threat*
3. *eliminate with extreme prejudice* (CIA)

> ● Capt. Robert Marasco claimed that he had what amounted to an official execution order from the CIA— an order to "eliminate with extreme prejudice."
>
> —*New York Times,* Apr. 18, 1971

4. *permanently remove from society*
5. *eliminate*

6. *neutralize*
7. *service the target* (DOD)

> • During Operation Desert Storm, one artillery captain was quoted as saying, "I prefer not to say we are killing other people. I prefer to say we are 'servicing the target.'"
> —*The New Doublespeak*

8. *attrit*
9. *forced involuntary disappearance*
10. *initiate a brutality event*
11. *snow the patient*

> • In some hospitals, "snowing the patient" means giving high doses of morphine—doses that are sometimes intentionally fatal for terminally ill patients.
> —*St. Paul* (MN) *Pioneer Press,* Aug. 10, 1992

land mine *n.*
popular armament

mercenary *n.*
1. *unilaterally controlled asset* (CIA)
2. *civilian irregular defense soldier* (DOD)

military withdrawal *n.*
backloading of augmentation personnel (DOD)

miss the target *v.*
1. *accidental delivery of ordnance equipment* (DOD)
2. *friendly fire* (DOD)
3. *incontinent ordnance* (DOD)
4. *outside current accuracy requirements* (DOD)

During the Vietnam war mercenaries were called "civilian irregular defense soldiers," refugees were "ambient non-combatant personnel," and enemy troops who survived bombing were "interdictional nonsuccumbers." Any sampan that was sunk was automatically a "waterborne logistic craft." Poisoning thousands of acres of vegetation with Agent Orange was a "resources control program" that produced "defoliation." American planes conducted "limited duration protective reactive strikes" with an "effective delivery of ordnance." When American troops attacked it was a "preemptive counterattack" or an "aggressive defense." Spraying an area with machine gun fire was "reconnaissance by fire." Sometimes American troops "engaged the enemy on all sides" (they were ambushed) and had to effect a "tactical redeployment" (they retreated). When American troops ambushed the enemy it was a "proactive counterattack."

- Missiles no longer "miss the target"; instead, they fall "outside current accuracy requirements."
  —*Quarterly Review of Doublespeak,* Jan. 1988

nerve gas *n.*
incapacitory agent (DOD)

neutron bomb *n.*
1. *enhanced radiation device*
2. *enlarged radiation weapon*
3. *cookie cutter* (DOD)

nuclear war *n.*
ultimate high intensity warfare (DOD)

other side attacks first *n.*
deliberate, unprovoked act of aggression

our side attacks first *n.*
1. *preemptive counterattack*
2. *preventive* or *preemptive action*
3. *offensive defense*

parachute *n.*
aerodynamic personnel decelerator

> • Even something as simple as a parachute has to
> have a complicated name.
> —*Philadelphia Inquirer,* July 15, 1973

peace *n.*
1. *permanent pre-hostility*
2. *temporary cessation of hostilities*

refugee *n.*
ambient noncombatant personnel

> • The military now calls refugees "ambient noncom-
> batant personnel."   —*Newsweek,* Apr. 15, 1984

retreat *n.*
1. *tactical deployment*
2. *backloading of augmentation personnel*
3. *redeployment*
4. *reconcentration*

shovel *n.*

1. *combat emplacement evacuator* (DOD)

> • A recent Defense Department publication calls a spade or a shovel a "combat emplacement evacuator."
> —*Philadelphia Inquirer,* July 15, 1973

2. *manually operated humus excavator*
3. *manually operated, minimally functioning earth displacer and remover*

> • Engineers at the Fort Belvoir, Virginia, Engineer School, define a shovel as a "manually operated, minimally functioning earth displacer and remover."
> —*Philadelphia Inquirer Magazine,* Mar. 21, 1993

sniper *n.*
long-range target reduction specialist (DOD)

steel nut *n.*
hexiform, rotatable surface compression unit (DOD)

For the Pentagon, it's not a plain, ordinary steel nut; it's a "hexiform rotatable surface compression unit," which is why it cost $2,043 for just one of them. So a piece of equipment "suffered dramatically degraded useful operational life owing to the fact that a $2,000 hexiform rotatable surface compression unit underwent catastrophic stress-related shaft detachment," which sounds a lot more impressive than saying it won't work because a 13-cent nut broke.
—*Christopher Cerf and Henry Beard*

SHOE

tent *n.*
frame-supported tension structure

> • The Navy is seeking "frame-supported tension structures for the Marine Corps Expeditionary Soft Shelter System." —*San Francisco Chronicle*, Sept. 11, 1985

theft *n.*
transfer

unneeded spare parts *n.*
inapplicable spare parts

war *n.*

1. *lethal intervention*
2. *defense*
3. *violence processing*
4. *police action*

   • The Korean War was not a war—it was a "police action."   —*The New Doublespeak*

5. *coercive diplomacy*

   • In scholarly journals, the preferred term for "war" is "coercive diplomacy."   —*Survival,* May/June 1987

"I believe you know Mars, God of Defense."

6. *an improbable compilation of dissimilar phenomena that, like the Cheshire cat, which seems to fade in and out as you look at it, leaving only its mocking smile, bedevils efforts at comprehension* (DOD)

> • The State Department, CIA and the Pentagon have produced a comprehensive study entitled "Joint Low-Intensity Conflict Project," which states that "low-intensity conflict is neither war nor peace. It is an improbable compilation of dissimilar phenomena that, like the Cheshire cat, which seems to fade in and out as you look at it, leaving only its mocking smile, bedevils efforts at comprehension."
>
> —*Philadelphia Inquirer,* Oct. 12, 1987

7. *violent peace*

> • The U.S. Navy calls the concept of low-intensity conflict "violent peace."   —*CBS News,* Feb. 20, 1984

War Department *n.*
Defense Department

warplane *n.*
threat platform

warship *n.*
threat platform

zipper *n.*
interlocking slide fastener

> • The Army calls a zipper an "interlocking slide fastener."   —*Quarterly Review of Doublespeak,* Apr. 1988

4
Death
and Taxes

....

assassinate *v.*
1. *neutralize*
2. *eliminate with extreme prejudice; see kill*

assassination *n.*
1. *irregular activities*
2. *total and complete immobilization*

> • Law enforcement officials in the Nixon administration once proposed the "total and complete immobilization" of General Manuel Antonio Noriega, who was at that time chief of intelligence in the Panama Defense Force. The Senate Intelligence Committee later discovered that this phrase was doublespeak for assassination. —*New York Times,* June 13, 1986

3. *permanently remove from society*

> • General Christoffel van der Westhizen of the South African Army proposed that the four black men opposed to apartheid be "permanently removed from society." Some days later, the men were found dead.
> —*New York Times,* Sept. 2, 1993

4. *executive action*

beaten to death *v.*

failed to survive interrogation

> ● ABC's "World News Tonight" for May 26, 1986 ran a report by Bob Zelnick from Jerusalem in which he reported that many Israelis were upset that Shin Beth [the Israeli internal police] was being given a bad name "just because two suspected terrorists failed to survive interrogation." An official investigation later revealed the two men had been beaten to death.
>
> —*In These Times,* June 25–July 8, 1986

cremation *n.*

after-death care

dead *mod.*

1. *not salvageable*

> ● When a sailor was transferred from the USS *Davidson* to the USS *Kitty Hawk,* he was very sick. In fact, his condition was "not salvageable," according to a Navy medical officer.
>
> —*Philadelphia Inquirer,* May 12, 1985

2. *nonviable*
3. *in a moribund state*

death *n.*

1. *negative patient care outcome*

> ● "Nothing in life is certain except Negative Patient Care Outcome and Revenue Enhancement."
>
> —Pye Chamberlayne, UPI Radio, as quoted by William Safire in the *New York Times Magazine,* Nov. 29, 1981

2. *terminal episode*

• At the thirty-six bed Community Hospital of the Valleys in Perris, California, twenty-four people died during six weeks, and all of them suffered the same "terminal episode." "We have found abnormal amounts of medication in several of the bodies," a coroner's investigator said.

—Philadelphia Inquirer, May 7, 1981

3. *substantive negative outcome*

• In anaesthesia journals it is common to report a death under anaesthesia as a "substantive negative outcome." *—Quarterly Review of Doublespeak*, July 1989

4. *immediate permanent incapacitation*

5. *terminal living*

• Soldiers who are hit by nuclear weapons during battle need not worry about dying a slow, painful death from radiation burns and vomiting. According to a U.S. Army field manual, they will merely sustain "immediate permanent incapacitation."

—Detroit (MI) *News*, Nov. 23, 1991

6. *adverse consequence* or *occurrence*

7. *mortality experience*

• "We never use the word 'death.' We tell a patient that you're about to have a mortality experience," said the doctor.

—Quarterly Review of Doublespeak, Apr. 1992

8. *systems failure*

9. *maximum incapacitation*

• In seeking the death penalty for four men accused of homicide, State Attorney Lawson Lamar said, "We are looking for maximum incapacitation for these people."

—St. Augustine (FL) *Record*, Dec. 3, 1992

10. *serious adverse effect*

> ● The Food and Drug Administration identified eighty-one "serious adverse effects," including thirty-eight deaths, from the use of E-Ferol Aqueous Solution. Death would certainly seem to be a serious adverse effect. —*New York Times,* May 2, 1984

11. *diagnostic misadventure of a high magnitude*
      see also *medical malpractice*
12. *unanticipated effect*
13. *meaningful consequence*
14. *transferred to ECU* (Eternal Care Unit)

death toll *n.*
1. *mortality rate*
2. *collateral damage*

die *v.*
1. *cease to breathe* or *CTB*
2. *patient failed to fulfill his wellness potential*

> ● The patient didn't die; he "failed to fulfill his wellness potential." —*Doublespeak*

3. *dialing down*

> ● Allowing the patient to die is called "dialing down." —*St. Paul* (MN) *Pioneer Press,* Aug. 10, 1992

dying *n.*
1. *failure to thrive* (FTT)
2. *dialing down;*
      see also *die*

euthanasia *n.*
death with dignity

grave *n.*
1. *underground condominium*
2. *eternal condominium*

high death toll *n.*
excess mortality rate

> ● Health officials are warning that a strain of
> influenza that caused a sharp rise in deaths in
> 1980–81 is appearing once again. But that's not how
> they said it. Instead, an epidemiologist for the Los
> Angeles County department of Heath Services said,
> "This is a strain that historically has been associated
> with some degrees of excess mortality."
> —*Santa Barbara (CA) News Press,* Jan. 10, 1988

morgue *n.*
regional forensic center

slaughter *n.*
1. *depopulation*

> ● When the Federal Government launched a program
> last fall to gas chickens—more than 7 million so far—in
> an effort to contain an influenza virus in Pennsylva-
> nia, it said it had "depopulated" the birds. "We use that
> terrible word depopulation to avoid saying slaughter,"
> explained a federal information officer.
> —*Quarterly Review of Doublespeak,* Apr. 1984

2. *purification*

> • Although the official media in Iran has reported the execution of several thousand people, Ayatollah Ruhollah Khomeini said that the prophet's wars were to purify nations and "those who prevent moral purification must be eliminated. In appearance this can seem like a mass killing to people, but in reality, it amounts to getting rid of obstacles to humanity. Iran purifies them if it can, or if not, it eliminates them."
>
> *—Los Angeles Times,* Jan. 14, 1982; as reported in *Inquiry Magazine,* Feb. 28, 1982

3. *ethnic cleansing*

tax *n.*

1. *passenger facility charge*

> • Don't call the fee airports levy on departing passengers a tax—it's a "passenger facility charge."
>
> *—The New Doublespeak*

2. *premium payment*
3. *user fee* or *charge*

> • In February of 1987, Budget Director James Miller insisted that the proposed budget did not contain tax increases. The budget contains "increased receipts" and "offsetting collections." Are these tax increases? "The answer is a definite no," declares Mr. Miller. The $1-per-ticket fee for airline and cruise tickets into and out of the U.S. is a "user charge," which will be applied toward the cost of running the U.S. Travel and Tourism Administration.   *—Wall Street Journal,* Jan. 9, 1987

4. *state collected revenue*
5. *wage-based premium*
see also *tax increase*

Airports levy a "passenger facility charge" on all departing passengers. So each time you board an airplane you pay $3 on top of the regular federal tax on your airplane ticket. Thus, on a round-trip flight from New York to Los Angeles with a change of planes in Chicago, you can pay up to $12 more. The money is supposed to go to improve airports, just like the $7 billion already collected from a tax on all airplane tickets. Congress and the various administrations, however, have refused to spend that $7 billion to improve airports, as is its stated purpose. Instead, they're using it to reduce the budget deficit.

So the "passenger facility charge" was instituted, a non-tax to be used to pay for the new and improved airport facilities that the airline ticket tax is supposed to pay for but doesn't, because Congress uses the airline ticket tax to reduce the deficit instead.

—*New York Times,* Mar. 20, 1990; *Philadelphia Inquirer,* Mar. 20, 1990; July 22, 1990

FRANK & ERNEST® by Bob Thaves

Frank & Ernest reprinted by permission of Newspaper Enterprise Association, Inc.

Shoe/By Jeff MacNelly

tax collector *n.*
Internal Revenue Service

tax evasion *n.*
account accommodation

> • Lawyers for Michael Milken argued that helping clients to evade taxes was just "account accommodation." —*Village Voice,* Feb. 23, 1993

tax increase *n.*

1. *revenue enhancement*

> • For the Reagan Administration, the phrase "tax increase" was replaced by the phrase "tax enhancement," and this in turn has been replaced by the phrase "revenue enhancement."
>
> —*Chicago Tribune*, Oct. 17, 1981

2. *recapture of benefits*

CLOUT ST.

3. *replacement of revenues*

> • When President Reagan raised taxes $99 billion in 1981, Republicans called it "revenue enhancement." When President Reagan said he would consider taxing Social Security benefits of the wealthy if Congress would not freeze cost-of-living expenses, Senator Robert Dole called it a "recapture of benefits," while White House spokesman Larry Speakes called the plan "replacement of revenues." Thus can President Reagan keep his promise that a tax increase would happen only "over my dead body."
>
> —*Seattle Times,* July 10, 1985

4. *increased receipts*
5. *offsetting collections*

> •In February of 1987, Budget Director James Miller insisted that the proposed budget did not contain tax increases. The budget contains "increased receipts" and "offsetting collections."
>
> —*Wall Street Journal,* Jan. 9, 1987

So much doublespeak is used in Japanese politics and so little of it is understood by the Japanese people that Kazuhisa Inoue, a member of the Japanese Diet (parliament), has asked the Japanese government to form a committee of linguists and other scholars to study ways to eliminate misleading language from parliamentary debate. Mr. Inoue has compiled a list of 51 expressions used regularly by Japanese politicians that ordinary Japanese cannot understand. Moreover, Mr. Inoue is concerned that such phrases used by Japanese officials in their dealings with foreign governments can lead to serious international misunderstandings.

When a Japanese Cabinet minister says "Eii doryoku shimasu" ("We shall make efforts"), other politicians know that he really means that he will do nothing. When a minister says he will accomplish something "kakyuteki sumiyaka" ("with the greatest expedition possible"), he really means that he will go as slow as possible. There are bureaucrats who say they will take "shoyo no gutaitkei sochi" ("necessary concrete measures"). Of course, that concrete isn't ever mixed and certainly is never poured. When a Japanese businessman says "Kangai saesete kudasai" ("Let me think about it"), he means no.

In 1969, Prime Minister Eisaku Sato visited the United States to assuage American anger over the flood of textile imports from Japan. During a meeting with Prime Minister Sato, President Nixon urged the Japanese to exercise restraint in their exports, to which Mr. Sato replied, "Zensho shimasu," which the translator dutifully rendered literally as "I will do my best." What Mr. Sato meant, of course, was "Not a chance." President Nixon, however, thought that Mr. Sato had agreed to limit Japanese textile exports to the United States. When Japan did not limit its textile exports, President Nixon was reportedly angry enough to call Mr. Sato a liar.

Keizo Obuchi, the Chief Cabinet Secretary and government spokesman, avoided comment on Mr. Inoue's proposal. But that was a good sign, because if Mr. Obuchi had said that it was difficult, he would really have been saying "Forget it." As long as politicians in any country can use doublespeak and get away with it, they will.

—*New York Times,* Mar. 27, 1988

6. *tax base erosion control*
7. *tax base broadening*

> • We all know that a tax increase is called "revenue enhancement." But now we have "tax base erosion control" and "tax base broadening."
>
> —*Quarterly Review of Doublespeak,* Oct. 1984

8. *user fee*

> • According to White House deputy press secretary Larry Speakes, it's not a gasoline tax but a "user fee" imposed "on those who use cars and gasoline."
>
> —*Philadelphia Inquirer,* Nov. 11, 1982

see also *tax*

9. *adjustment of a windfall*
10. *temporary minimal adjustment*
11. *receipt proposals*
12. *receipts strengthening*

> • Some elected officials have decided to call a tax increase "receipts strengthening" or "receipts proposals."   —*The New Doublespeak*

13. *update the revenue mechanism*

> • "The latest words from Washington include 'update the revenue mechanism,' which means a tax increase."
>
> —*New York Times,* Sept. 16, 1982

14. *contribute*

> • President Bill Clinton said that ". . . more Americans must contribute today so that all Americans can do better tomorrow."   —*New York Times,* Feb. 16, 1993

15. *pay your fair share*

> ● President Clinton said, "I'll ask the wealthiest Americans to pay their fair share."
>
> —*New York Times,* Feb. 16, 1993

temporary coffins *n.*
aluminum transfer cases (DOD)

5

Crimes and Misdemeanors

....

bribe *n.*

1. *rebate*
2. *discount*
3. *instance of the free market at work*

> ● Frederic Andre of the Interstate Commerce Commission said that the Commission should not worry about bribes in the trucking business because bribes are "one of the clearest instances of the free market at work . . . they are just discounts. . . . A bribe is a rebate, is it not?" —*Philadelphia Inquirer*, Dec. 22, 1982

4. *fee for product testing*

> ● Federal investigators discovered that in the heart pacemaker industry, bribes and kickbacks are called rebates and fees for product testing.
> —*Philadelphia Inquirer*, July 25, 1982

5. *sales incentive*
6. *after-sales service*

> ● According to a report on CNN, kickbacks are simply "after-sales services."
> —*Quarterly Review of Doublespeak*, Oct. 1991

7. *physician practice enhancement* or *physician bonding*

> • The word "kickback" isn't fashionable among hospital administrators. They prefer to say "physician practice enhancement" or "physician bonding."
> —*Wall Street Journal*, Dec. 27, 1988

8. *normal gratitude*
9. *incentive payment*
10. *sales credit*
11. *goodwill gesture*
12. *gratuity*
13. *access to the system*

burglar alarm *n.*
intrusion detection device (DOD)

burglary *n.*
1. *intelligence gathering operation* (FBI)
2. *unconsented physical search* (CIA)

Non Sequitur

© 1998 Washington Post Writers Group. Reprinted with permission.

conflict of interest *n.*
dual commitment

> ● "Perhaps part of the difficulty with 'conflict of inter-
> est' lies in the phrase itself, which has disparaging
> connotations. *The Annals of Internal Medicine* uses
> the term 'dual commitment' and asks authors to dis-
> close these to editors. *The Lancet*'s policy is much the
> same." —*The Lancet,* May 19, 1997

crime *n.*
1. *inappropriate action* or *behavior*
2. *failure to comply with the law*
3. *antisocial* or *dysfunctional behavior*
4. *ethical lapse*
5. *judgmental lapse*

death penalty *n.*
maximum incapacitation

> ● State Attorney Lawson Lamar said, "We are looking
> for maximum incapacitation for these people." He is
> seeking the death penalty for four men accused of
> homicide. —*St. Augustine* (FL) *Record,* Dec. 3, 1992

death row *n.*
1. *capital sentence unit*

> ● Trenton State Prison no longer has a death house;
> now it's the "capital sentences unit."
> —*New York Times,* June 7, 1983

2. *unit for condemned persons*

> • We know, of course, that it is no longer "jail" or "prison." So, at the Green Haven Correctional Facility in Stormville, New York, it is no longer "Death Row" but the "Unit for Condemned Persons."
>
> —*Village Voice,* July 26, 1983

In the semantic environment of law, "no" can mean "yes"—at least that was the case in Pennsylvania not too long ago. When a woman brought rape charges against a man for forcing her to engage in sex with him, the charges were dropped when the prosecutor said the woman had protested only with words. The woman had said "no" and "don't do that" repeatedly, but she had not physically tried to protect herself. Under a ruling by the Pennsylvania Supreme Court, saying "no" is not enough to sustain a rape charge. So in the state of Pennsylvania, "no" means "yes" in the language of sex.

—*Philadelphia Inquirer,* July 27, 1994

destroy evidence *v.*

1. *correct a management deficiency*

> • When it was discovered that the United States Information Agency had a blacklist of Americans who were considered too liberal to be invited to speak overseas by the USIA, an official at the USIA said the blacklist might not be a crime, but it was "an inappropriate management practice." Thomas Harvey, the general counsel of the USIA, ordered subordinates to destroy over seven hundred documents explaining how the list

was prepared and then said he wasn't destroying evidence; he just wanted "to correct a management deficiency."   *—Philadelphia Inquirer,* Mar. 1, 1984

2. *exclude irrelevant documents*
3. *clean up the historical record*

drug deal *n.*
narcotic event

> • Explaining why he supported the death penalty for drug dealers, Vice President Bush referred to the murders committed during a "narcotic event."
> *—Wall Street Journal,* Oct. 21, 1988

drug dealer *n.*
drug enterprise leader

> • The New Hampshire legislature is considering a bill that would increase penalties for "drug enterprise leaders."   *—Boston Globe,* Jan. 10, 1988

execution *n.*
1. *lethal intervention*
2. *permanent incapacitation*

executioner *n.*
execution technician

> • The bill making lethal injection New Jersey's official method of capital punishment states that the prisoners are to be put to death by "execution technicians" since the New Jersey Medical Society is opposed to cooperation in executions by physicians.
> *—New York Times,* June 7, 1983

In *Burdick v. Takushi*, the U.S. Supreme Court ruled that despite the sacredness of the ballot, despite the basic and important nature of voting, your vote doesn't count if it's a write-in vote and that city, state, county or other jurisdiction has a law banning write-in votes.

According to the Supreme Court, you do not have "a fundamental right to vote for any particular candidate." You are "simply guaranteed an equal voice in the election of those who govern."
—*Burdick v. Takushi*
112 S. Ct. 2039 (1992)

fraud *n.*
mistake

● After the states of California and New Jersey charged Sears Auto Centers with car repair fraud, Sears said that it had canceled the sales incentive program that had "created an environment where mistakes did occur." Then, in a series of national advertisements, Sears acknowledged that "mistakes have occurred" at its auto centers. Perhaps Sears should consult a legal dictionary to learn that fraud is not a mistake but a result of intentional action.
—*Courant* (Hartford, CT), June 26, 1992

illegal *mod.*
inappropriate

● White-collar crime is sometimes referred to as "inappropriate" behavior—especially after it has been discovered.   —*New York Times*, Sept. 21, 1988

illegal alien *n.*
undocumented worker

imprisoned *mod.*
tactically immobilized

> • According to syndicated columnist Georgie Anne Geyer, an imprisoned opposition journalist was said by the Philippines government to be "tactically immobilized."   —*Seattle Times*, Aug. 30, 1983

infanticide *n.*
giving the baby a bath

> • In China, female infanticide by drowning is called "giving the baby a bath."
> —*Miami Herald*, Sept. 26, 1991

intention *n.*
conscious objective

> • One's state of mind is intentional as to one's conduct or the result of one's conduct if such conduct or result is one's conscious objective.
> —*Meadville* (PA) *Tribune*, Nov. 28, 1986

jail *n.*
See *prison*

jail sentence *n.*
placement in a long-term structured environment

lie detector test *n.*
forensic psychophysiological detection of deception test, or *PDDT* (DOD)

Mafia *n.*
career-offender cartel

Mafioso *n.*
member of a career-offender cartel

> • The New Jersey Division of Gaming Enforcement, in
> a report to the Casino Control Commission, did not use
> the terms "Mafia" or "Cosa Nostra." Instead, the report
> refers to a "member of a career-offender cartel."
> *—Philadelphia Inquirer,* Jan. 5, 1979

pedophilia *n.*
intergenerational intimacy

police who stop you and demand identification *n.*
consensual encounter

> • According to a recent U.S. Supreme Court ruling, a
> person stopped on the street by police, questioned, and
> ordered to produce identification has not been seized
> but is merely engaged in a "consensual encounter."
> *—Los Angeles Times,* Feb. 21, 1990

prison *n.*
1. *labor reform camp for ideological re-education*

> • Since there is no crime in North Korea, there are no
> prisons, but there *are* "labor reform camps for ideolog-
> ical re-education."
> *—Quarterly Review of Doublespeak,* Jan. 1988

2. *correctional facility* or *institution*
3. *secure facility*
4. *adult detention center*

Imagine that you're waiting for friends to meet you. You're sitting on the hood of a car in your neighborhood when two police officers pass by. One of the officers asks if that's your car. "No," you reply. "Then why are you sitting on it?" asks the officer. "I'm just waiting for some friends to pick me up, so we can go shoot some pool," you say. "Then where's your pool stick? How can you shoot pool without a pool stick?" the officer asks. You're about to point out that the pool hall has lots of pool cues to use and you never wanted to own your own cue anyway, but before you can say anything the officers move closer and ask you to show them some identification.

What do you do? Do you refuse and walk away? That's what you're supposed to do, according to a California ruling *(California v. Lopez)* left standing by the U.S. Supreme Court. According to the Court you are involved in a "consensual encounter," meaning that the police don't have any right to detain you, so you can walk away at any time. So, if the police stop you on the street, question you and order you to produce identification, you are merely engaged in a "consensual encounter" and are not entitled to any Constitutional protections against warrantless searches and seizures.

Sheriff's deputies in Fort Lauderdale, Florida, took their lead from the Supreme Court and created a technique they call "working the buses." They wait at rest stops on the interstate highway for long distance buses. When the buses stop, the deputies board the bus, walk down the aisle and, without any reason to suspect any passenger of anything, ask passengers questions and whether they can search their luggage. If you were a passenger and they asked you, would you refuse?

According to the Supreme Court in *Florida v. Bostick* (212 Cal. App. 3d 289 [1989]; 111 S. Ct. 2382 [1991]), you can say no because this is another "consensual encounter" and the search is a "consensual search." Of course, the deputies don't tell you that you have a right to refuse. Riders have testified that they thought they would be taken off the bus if they refused to cooperate, so they cooperated. The Court's use of "consensual" in both these cases gives a whole new meaning to the word, a meaning that could have interesting implications in the relations between men and women, employers and employees, and a whole range of relationships.

• The Fairfax County, Virginia, courthouse is now called the Fairfax County Judicial Center. Behind the judicial center is the Fairfax County Adult Detention Center, which used to be called the county jail.

—*Quarterly Review of Doublespeak,* Jan. 1989

ransom *n.*
payment for services rendered

• Ransom isn't paid to kidnappers, but a "contribution is made" to cover abduction expenses, or there were "payments for services rendered."

—*Quarterly Review of Doublespeak,* Jan. 1988

riot *n.*
civil disorder

riot control *n.*
confrontation management

riot police *n.*
crowd management team

• Members of the Metro Toronto Police public order unit are not the riot squad. They are the "crowd management team."

—*The Globe and Mail* (Toronto), May 9, 1992

shot by the police *n.*
legal intervention

• The fourth highest cause of death among African-American males in the U.S. is "homicide/legal intervention."

—Paul Reis, et al., eds., *The American Woman 1992–93: A Status Report,* Norton, 1992

solitary confinement *n.*
1. *individual behavior adjustment unit*
2. *involuntary administrative segregation*
3. *therapeutic segregation*

stolen goods *n.*
temporarily displaced inventory

torture *n.*
1. *in-depth interrogation*
2. *physical pressure*

> • The commission headed by Israeli Supreme Court Justice Moshe Landau, which investigated the crime of the Shin Bet security agency, issued a report in which they justified the use of "physical pressure" in certain instances when interrogating suspects. The Israeli cabinet then formed a committee to consider the amount of "physical force" Israeli security agents may use in questioning Palestinians suspected of guerrilla actions.
> —*Philadelphia Inquirer,* Nov. 9, 1987

3. *special interrogation procedures*
4. *exceptional measures*
5. *inappropriate physical abuse*

> • A mental patient in a straitjacket at the Creedmoor Psychiatric Center in New York died of "inappropriate physical abuse," said Irene Platt, acting chair of the New York State Commission on Quality of Care for the Mentally Disabled.   —*New York Times,* Apr. 25, 1984

unlawful *mod.*
inappropriate

When the Hasbro toy company started importing G.I. Joe action figures, the U.S. Customs people were not amused. Dolls are subject to an import tariff, claimed the customs people. These aren't dolls, replied Hasbro. They're action figures, because these are for boys to play with. Since boys don't play with dolls, these can't be dolls, so they must be action figures. After an eight-year court battle, Hasbro's version of reality lost to the U.S. Customs version, and G.I. Joe dolls are now subject to the import tariff on dolls. Hasbro pays the tariff, but it still puts the label "action figure" on G.I. Joe and calls Joe an "action figure" in all its advertising.

—*Time,* July 31, 1989

warden (OF A PRISON) *n.*
superintendent or *supervisor*

Hagar the Horrible

Reprinted with special permission of King Features Syndicate.

6

Health
and Welfare

alcoholic *n.*
1. *chemically unfortunate*
2. *victim of habitually detrimental lifestyle*

amphetamines *n.*
activity boosters

bag (OF ICE CUBES) *n.*
thermal therapy kit

> • In the doublespeak of hospital bills, a "thermal therapy" kit is a bag of ice cubes, and a plastic cup is a "urinal." —*New York Times*, Jan. 27, 1993

bald *mod.*
hair disadvantaged

> • Men in Japan aren't bald; they're hair disadvantaged. —*Japan Economic Journal*, Mar. 16, 1991

bathtub *n.*
body cleaning system

bum *n.*
non-goal-oriented member of society

decapitation *n.*
surgical isolation of the head

diet *n.*
1. *nutritional avoidance therapy*

> ● People don't go on diets these days; now it's called "nutritional avoidance therapy."
> —*Detroit Free Press*, Jan. 11, 1988

2. *caloric reduction program*

drop a baby *v.*
nonfacile manipulation of newborn

drown *v.*
subaquate

A poll taken in 1990 by the National Opinion Research Center of the University of Chicago found that only 24 percent of those surveyed thought more money should be spent on "welfare," but 68 percent were willing to spend more on "assistance for the poor." Likewise, those surveyed were willing to spend more for "national defense" and "assistance to other countries," but they were not willing to spend more on "the military" or "foreign aid."

—*Liberal Opinion Week*, Sept. 3, 1990

drug addict *n.*

1. *substance abuser*
2. *person with chemical dependency disorder*

> ● Four Winds, a private psychiatric hospital in Saratoga Springs, New York, doesn't treat addicts. It treats "persons with chemical dependency disorders."
> *—Quarterly Review of Doublespeak,* Apr. 1992

drug addiction *n.*

1. *pharmaceutical preference*
2. *the interrelationship of a drug with the human body*

> ● The doctor said that "drug addiction is too strong a word." Rather, he said, the drug had "established an interrelationship with the body, such that if the drug is removed precipitously, there is a reaction."
> *—Philadelphia Inquirer,* Jan. 6, 1982

3. *substance abuse*

> ● If you're not sure whether the problem is alcoholism or drug addiction, you can just use the term "substance abuse."
> *—Quarterly Review of Doublespeak,* Jan. 1988

4. *chemical dependency*

drug test *n.*
physical examination

drunk *mod.*
in a nonsober condition

• The ITAR-Tass news agency reported that a U.S. diplomat in Moscow was in a "non-sober condition" at the time of the automobile accident.
—*The Olympian* (Olympia, WA), May 17, 1993

electric razor *n.*
hair removal system

emergency *n.*
non-routine operation

eyeglasses *n.*
eyewear

false teeth *n.*
compensated edentia

• Thanks to the miracle of advertising, you don't have to wear false teeth anymore. Now you can wear "compensated edentia."
—*Freeway News* (Minneapolis), Sept. 21, 1988

fat *mod.*
voluminous

• AerInter of France requires two tickets for anyone taking up two seats "whether they be injured or voluminous."
—*San Diego Union*, 1991

fat person *n.*
calorically disadvantaged

girdle *n.*
1. *form persuader*

2. *body shaper*
3. *antigravity panties*

> • Now women can buy "anti-gravity panties," other-wise known as girdles.
> —*Quarterly Review of Doublespeak*, July 1988

4. *shapewear*
5. *de-emphasizer*
6. *outerwear enhancer*

gymnasium *n.*
human resource laboratory

handicapped *mod.*
1. *physically challenged*
2. *differently abled*

> • *The New York Yellow Pages* lists a telephone number for "Services for the Differently Abled."
> —*Quarterly Review of Doublespeak*, July 1988

3. *person with differing abilities*

harm *v.*
induce an adverse reaction

hospital *n.*
wellness center

insanity *n.*
mental activity at the margins

> • According to author Kate Millett, insanity should be seen as "mental activity at the margins."
> —*Philadelphia Inquirer*, Mar. 6, 1992

"Love it! 'People of smoke' instead of 'Smokers.'"

kill (HUMANS) *v.*
snow the patient

> • In some hospitals, "snowing the patient" means giv-
> ing high doses of morphine—doses that are sometimes
> intentionally fatal for terminally ill patients.
> —*St. Paul* (MN) *Pioneer Press,* Aug. 10, 1992

medical malpractice *n.*

1. *diagnostic misadventure of a high magnitude*

> ● The surgeon accidentally perforated the patient's colon, and the resulting complications caused the patient's death. The death was attributed, however, to a "diagnostic misadventure of a high magnitude."
>
> —*Philadelphia Inquirer,* Apr. 24, 1988

2. *therapeutic misadventure*

> ● After a series of surgical mistakes, including slitting a patient's throat accidentally during surgery, surgeons at the Martin Luther King, Jr./Drew Medical Center in Watts lost the patient. "It was a chain of stupidity and incompetence the likes of which I've never seen," said Dr. Elias Amador, chief of the department of pathology. The cause of death, according to the Los Angeles county coroner, was a "therapeutic misadventure"—a common term in medical doublespeak.
>
> —*Los Angeles Times,* Sept. 3, 1989

mentally ill people *n.*

mental health consumers

> ● At a conference, former mentally ill patients referred to themselves as "mental health consumers."
>
> —*Orlando Sentinel,* Mar. 15, 1988

nanny *n.*

interface with the children in a habitual way

> ● An adviser to the Prime Minister of Canada said that the Prime Minster's children did not have a nanny. However, there was a household staff member who "interfaced with the children in a habitual way."
>
> —*Vancouver Sun,* Nov. 22, 1984

"We do not have the homeless, people from inner cities, and abused women eating hospitality meals and living in shelters. We have poor people from ghettos, including beaten women and their children, eating in soup kitchens and living in poorhouses."

—*Philadelphia Inquirer,* Nov. 8, 1988

old *mod.*

1. *chronologically challenged*

   • "You're not getting older. You're chronologically challenged" proclaims the ad for bifocal eyeglasses.

   —*Star-Ledger* (Newark, NJ), Apr. 29, 1993

2. *used*

old people *n.*

1. *chronologically gifted citizens*

   • Old people don't live in a retirement community anymore. Now they live in "a senior congregate living community for the chronologically gifted."

   —*Philadelphia Inquirer,* Dec. 15, 1989

2. *chronologically experienced citizens*

   • It's not "the elderly" or "senior citizens" anymore. Now it's "chronologically experienced citizens."

   The News Journal (Daytona, FL), Jan. 12, 1988

outhouse *n.*

natural amenity unit

pain *n.*
1. *discomfort*
2. *slight pressure*

painful *mod.*
mildly uncomfortable

paranoia *n.*
hypervigilance

patient *n.*
compromised susceptible host

> • Nurses no longer treat sick people in the hospital. Now a patient is called "a compromised susceptible host."   —*Quarterly Review of Doublespeak,* Oct. 1988

pet *n.*
1. *animal companion*

> • Pets aren't just pets anymore; they're "animal companions."
> —*U.S. News and World Report,* July 22, 1991

2. *companion animal*

> • If pets are really "companion animals," must we now go to "companion animal stores" to buy goldfish?
> —*Harper's Magazine,* Aug. 1988

poor *mod.*
1. *economically disadvantaged*
2. *psychosocially and culturally deprived*

poor people *n.*

1. *fiscal underachievers*

> • A former Florida state senator confessed that when he was in office, he frequently referred to "fiscal underachievers," not the poor.
>
> —*Quarterly Review of Doublespeak*, Apr. 1987

2. *impoverished underclass*
3. *economically marginalized* or *nonaffluent nonaffluent*

> • Poor people aren't really "poor"; they're economically marginalized. —*Christianity Today*, Sept. 2, 1988

4. *disadvantaged*
5. *deprived elements*

poverty *n.*

1. *low income*
2. *low-income circumstances*

> • In Canada, there are no poor children, just children in "low-income circumstances."
>
> —*Toronto Star*, Jan. 22, 1990

3. *economic deprivation*

public lavatory *n.*
guest relations facility

retirement community *n.*

1. *senior congregate living community for the chronologically gifted*

> • Old people don't live in a retirement community anymore. Now they live in "a senior congregate living community for the chronologically gifted."
>
> —*Philadelphia Inquirer*, Dec. 15, 1989

2. *adult congregate living facility*
3. *disengagement community*

root canal *n.*
endodontic therapy

scared *mod.*
philosophically challenged or *disillusioned*

smell *v.*
organoleptic analysis

> • A magazine published by the Food and Drug Administration noted that decomposition in shellfish "is detected by organoleptic analysis," or smelling them.   —*New York Times,* Jan. 3, 1986

smell good *v.*
make a positive odor statement

> • People today are "using fragrance to cover other personal smells, or as one advertisement put it, to 'make a positive odor statement.'"
> —*Atlanta Weekly,* Oct. 9, 1988

spanking *n.*
intense adverse intervention

> • Family counselors describe spanking children as "intense adverse intervention."
> —*Houston Chronicle,* Jan. 10, 1988

spoiled *mod.*
distressed

• The owner of a fruit and vegetable market in Seattle, Washington, said that "from time to time we do take advantage of particular lots of distressed produce that we can sort and offer inexpensively to our customers."
—*Seattle Times*, Nov. 19, 1984

stink *v.*
exceed the odor threshold

• To some, sludge does not stink; rather, it "exceeds the odor threshold."   —*The New Doublespeak*

stupid *mod.*
intuitively counterproductive

surgery *n.*
invasive procedure

• Doctors don't call it surgery; they call it an "invasive procedure."
—*Quarterly Review of Doublespeak*, Oct. 1988

toothbrush *n.*
1. *home plaque removal instrument*

• The advertisement is for a "home plaque removal instrument," or a toothbrush, as it's more commonly known.   —*Quarterly Review of Doublespeak*, Apr. 1988

2. *oral hygiene appliance*

toothpaste *n.*
oral cleansing product

unconscious *mod.*

to be in non-decision-making form

> President Reagan was in "non-decision-making form for two or three hours after the injection," said the doctor.   —*Washington Post*, Feb. 11, 1988

vomit *n.*

protein spill

> Some of the amusement rides at Expo 86 in Vancouver, Canada, are so exciting that officials at the park expect "the occasional protein spill." An official said the term was coined after staff members had difficulty explaining exactly what happened when radioing for assistance.
> —*Quarterly Review of Doublespeak*, Apr. 1986

7

The Workplace

bonus payment *n.*
motivational reward

break *v.*
render inoperative

briefcase *n.*
data transport system

demotion *n.*
negative advancement

> • Hard times have hit the television industry. . . . "Cost
> containment" (a slashed budget) could lead to "nega-
> tive advancement" (you trade jobs with the janitor).
> —*TV Guide*, Mar. 21–27, 1987

desk *n.*
individual screened workstation

employee *n.*

1. *associate*
2. *developmental resource*
3. *partner*
4. *team member*
5. *human resource*
6. *human factor*
7. *human capital*

employees only *n.*
Unqualified Persons Forbidden

> • A sign on a door in a Lake Tahoe, Nevada, hotel: "Unqualified Persons Forbidden."
> —*Quarterly Review of Doublespeak,* Jan. 1989

fire (EMPLOYEES) *v.*

1. *downsize*
2. *dehire*
3. *deselect*
4. *destaff*
5. *de-employ*
6. *disemploy*
7. *derecruit*
8. *right size*
9. *correct size*

> • You might have been the wrong size; more likely, once you've been "correct sized," you're out of a job.
> —*The New Doublespeak*

10. *re-engineer*

> • "Work re-engineering" is, for some, preferable to "laying off workers."   —*The New Doublespeak*

11. *outplace*
12. *select out*
13. *release*
14. *excess*
15. *non-retain*
16. *displace*
17. *idle indefinitely*

> • The LTV Corporation called the layoff of 600 workers an "indefinite idling," so it wouldn't have to pay severance or pension benefits.
> —*Wall Street Journal*, May 22, 1985

> • In 1987 General Motors included a plant-closing moratorium in its contract with the United Automobile Workers. GM then proceeded to close four plants, calling the closing "indefinite idlings" that weren't covered by the moratorium. In 1990, GM officials wondered why the union officials didn't trust them during contract negotiations.
> —*Wall Street Journal*, Aug. 29, 1990

18. *involuntarily separate*

> • Bell Labs once chose to "involuntarily separate" 140 workers from the payroll.
> —*New York Times*, July 12, 1984

19. *separate from the job*
20. *negotiate the departure of*
21. *reduce surplus personnel*
22. *eliminate positions*
23. *retire prematurely*
24. *redeploy*
25. *redirect*
26. *eliminate redundancies in the human resources area*

27. *reorganize*
28. *replace*
29. *request departure*
30. *reduce in force* or *RIF*
31. *selectively separate*
32. *adjust the skill mix*
33. *transition*
34. *relocate vocationally*
35. *adjust* or *realign* or *rebalance the workforce*
36. *correct a workforce imbalance*
37. *implement a volume-related production schedule adjustment*
38. *implement a career assessment and redeployment*
39. *implement a career transition*
40. *implement a lean concept of synchronous organizational structures*

> • General Motors of Canada conceded that their "lean concept of synchronous organizational structures" would result in layoffs.   —*The New Doublespeak*

41. *implement involuntary methodologies*
42. *implement an employment security policy*
43. *implement a Voluntary Window Incentive Program*

> • As part of its attempts to restructure and downsize, the *Baltimore Sun* implemented a "Voluntary Window Incentive Program" rather than actually "fire" its employees.   —*The New Doublespeak*

44. *change the chemistry*
45. *cull executives*
46. *coerce transition*
47. *degrow*

48. *deploy*
49. *release resources*
50. *uninstall*

> • At one computer company, you might find yourself "uninstalled," not fired.   —*The New Doublespeak*

51. *cease production*
52. *eliminate positions*
53. *strengthen global effectiveness*
54. *transition*
55. *offer voluntary severance*
56. *declare excess to requirements*
57. *refocus the company's skills set*

> • One company, after laying off 10 percent of its workforce, referred to the layoffs as a "refocusing of the company's skill set."   —*The New Doublespeak*

58. *reposition*
59. *reduce duplication*
60. *focus reduction*

> • Tandem Computers refers to downsizing in their company as "reducing duplication" or "focused reduction."   —*The New Doublespeak*

61. *reshape*
62. *adjust the payroll*
63. *change the chemistry*
64. *consolidate operations*
65. *undertake a major repositioning*

> • Varian Associates of Palo Alto, California, chose to "undertake a major repositioning" and reduce its workforce.   —*The New Doublespeak*

66. *scale down a duplicative workforce*
67. *involuntarily separate from the workforce*
68. *offer a severance package offer*
69. *improve operations*
70. *reposition employees*
71. *offer a career-change opportunity*

> ●"This was not a cutback or a layoff. It was a career-change opportunity," said the president of Clifford of Vermont, Inc.   —*Valley News* (CT), May 3, 1990

72. *adjust work schedules*
73. *terminate voluntarily*
74. *resign voluntarily*
75. *implement a force management program*
76. *reduce an imbalance of forces* or *skills*
77. *unassign*

> ● AT&T once implemented a "force management program" aimed at "reducing an imbalance of forces or skills." The 40,000 workers who were "unassigned" were forced to look elsewhere for employment.
> —*The New Doublespeak*

78. *assign candidates for derecruitment to a mobility pool*
79. *place executives on special assignment*
80. *reduce the headcount*

> ● Harris Bank of Chicago "rightsized" by "reducing the headcount," thus reducing its payroll costs.
> —*The New Doublespeak*

81. *retain employees negatively*
82. *request departure*
83. *selectively improve operational capacity*
84. *manage staff resources down*

• "We don't characterize it as a layoff," said a Sun Oil Company spokesman. "We're managing our staff resources. Sometimes you manage them up and sometimes you manage them down."

—*Philadelphia Inquirer*, Dec. 19, 1985

85. *surplus workers*
86. *correct force imbalances*
87. *non-assign*
88. *rationalize costs*
89. *a redirection to focus on customer service*
90. *being walked*

> • When an employee is walked to the Human Resources Department and instructed never to return to his or her office.
>
> —*The Ragan Report*, Aug. 23, 1993

91. *adjust the workforce complement*
92. *negative employee retention*
93. *involuntary downward deployment*
94. *accelerate the special attrition program*
95. *census reduction*

> • In Canadian government doublespeak, laying off workers becomes "census reductions made necessary by rising costs."   —*Toronto Star*, Oct. 14, 1990

96. *complement adjustment*

> • When the Pennsylvania Public Welfare Department laid off 900 workers, it was called a "complement adjustment."   —*Philadelphia Inquirer*, May 12, 1980

lay off workers *v.*
See *fire*

mining company *n.*
extractive industry

> ● They're not mining companies anymore; they're "extractive industries."
>
> —*Albuquerque* (NM) *Journal*, Jan. 10, 1988

overtime *n.*
off-hours work

repair department *n.*
Customer Engineering

staple *n.*
resin-coated power fastener

unemployed *mod.*
1. *waiting to be employed*
2. *between jobs*

© Tribune Media Services. All rights reserved. Reprinted with permission.

Question: When is a decrease in competition an increase in competition? Answer: When the Federal Communications Commission says it is. The FCC adopted new regulations that allow a single corporation to own 30 AM and 30 FM stations, a substantial increase from the previous limit of 12 and 12. Moreover, the new rules allow one corporation to dominate up to 25 percent of a single large market, and there is no limit on how much of a smaller market one corporation may control. The new rules also permit joint ventures among competing corporations, allowing them to share programs and thus control large segments of selected markets. The FCC said that this action supports its aim of increasing competition and diversity in programming "by recognizing that the existence of a vibrant marketplace is necessary to maximize those goals."

—*Business Week,* June 29, 1992;
Philadelphia Inquirer, Apr. 11, 1992;
Apr. 18, 1992

8

Government and Politics

....

blockade *n.*
sanctions with teeth

bomb *n.*
entry device

> ● The Philadelphia police used an "entry device" composed of 4.5 pounds of explosive. The resulting explosion and fire killed eleven people and destroyed 61 homes.
> —*Philadelphia Inquirer,* July 31, 1985; Aug. 1, 1985

budget cut *n.*
1. *internal reallocation*
2. *institutional self-help*

> ● Cutting salaries or laying off workers are both examples of "institutional self-help," or budget cuts.
> —*Education Week,* Nov. 29, 1989

3. *negative base adjustment*

4. *productivity increases*

> • The Illinois Board of Higher Education uses the following terminology: "internal reallocation," "institutional self-help," "negative base adjustment," "productivity increases" and "personal services." All mean "budget cuts."   *—UPI Faculty Action,* Nov.–Dec. 1982

5. *negative growth*
6. *advanced downward adjustments*
7. *correction*

> • When Rutgers University cut 25 percent of the non-instructional budget in the middle of the school year, it was called a "mid-year budget correction."
> *—Quarterly Review of Doublespeak,* Oct. 1983

8. *carefully targeted reform*
9. *cost containment*

budget surplus *n.*

1. *positive cash balance*
2. *potential cash margin*

> • Governor Cuomo of New York didn't want to say that the state had a big and growing budget surplus. Instead, he used such words as "a positive cash balance" and "potential cash margin." At one point, the phrase "positive margin" was "floating around but wasn't used."   *—New York Times,* Nov. 1, 1984

capital gains tax reduction *n.*
targeted job-creation deductions

chicken coop *n.*
single-purpose agricultural structure

> • The proposed tax simplification law includes a special tax depreciation break for "single-purpose agricultural structures," or what are more commonly called chicken coops and pigpens.
> —*Philadelphia Inquirer,* Aug. 21, 1986

committee (TO PLAN ASSASSINATIONS) *n.*
Health Alteration Committee

> • Earlier in the history of the CIA, the committee that planned the assassination of foreign leaders was called the "Health Alteration Committee."
> —*In These Times,* Nov. 15–21, 1989

congressional pay raise *n.*
pay equalization concept

> • The U.S. Senate did not vote itself a $23,200 pay raise in the dead of night. According to Senator Ted Stevens of Alaska, "It is not a pay raise. It is a pay equalization concept."
> —*Los Angeles Times,* July 18, 1991

congressional pork barrel *n.*
congressional projects of national significance

> • The $153 billion transportation bill in Congress includes $11 billion for pork barrel projects that are called "congressional projects of national significance."
> —*Philadelphia City Paper,* Aug. 16, 1991

congressional recess *n.*
1. *district work period*

In New York, in 1912, a voter became upset when the candidate for whom he voted ignored all the promises he had made during the campaign once he was in office. The voter sued the politician for breach of oral contract: After all, reasoned the disillusioned voter, weren't the promises made by a politician during a campaign a promise to the voters? Didn't those same oral promises constitute an oral contact between the candidate and the voter, a contract in which in exchange for the voter's vote the candidate promised to do certain things if elected?

Unfortunately, the judge ruled that "a contract cannot be based on an ante-election promise to voters generally by a candidate for public office, so as to give a voter a right to restrain the promisor from violating same." In other words, there's no legal way voters can make politicians keep their promises once they have been elected, so politicians are free to say whatever they want during an election campaign and then do whatever they want once they're in office.

—*O'Reilly v. Mitchell*, 85 Misc. 176, 148 N.Y.S. 88 (Sup. Ct. 1914)

• When reporters laughed at the term "Independence Day District Work Period," House majority leader Thomas S. Foley said, "I don't know why you always laugh when we say that. We used to call it a recess, but you kept calling it a vacation. So we changed the name to district work period, and you still call it a vacation."

—*New York Times,* July 7, 1988;
Hartford (CT) *Courant,* July 15, 1988

2. *nonlegislative period*

cow (ALSO CHICKEN AND PIG) *n.*

1. *grain-consuming animal unit* (USDA)

> • The U.S. Department of Agriculture, in its monthly feed outlook report, refers to cows, chickens, pigs, and other farm animals as "grain-consuming animal units" (or GCAUs).
>
> *—Quarterly Review of Doublespeak,* July 1988

2. *bovine unit*

deficiency *n.*
shortfall

> • William Graham, NASA's acting administrator, said, "With the loss of Challenger, we have lost one quarter of our shuttle fleet and are in temporary hiatus of shuttle flights. It is certain that we will have a shortfall in the national launch capability in the near term."
>
> *—Orlando* (FL) *Sentinel,* Mar. 2, 1986

discrimination *n.*
disparate negative impact

emergency vehicle *n.*
major incident response unit

exit *n.*
that part of a means of egress that leads to an entrance to an exit

> • A government pamphlet on fire prevention in homes for the elderly offers the following definition: "Exit access is that part of a means of egress that leads to an entrance to an exit."
>
> *—Quarterly Review of Doublespeak,* Apr. 1988

The more things change, the more they stay the same—and no place is this dictum more true than in politics. Consider these two speeches by two quite different presidents. On July 27, 1981, President Ronald Reagan said in a speech televised to the American public that "I will not stand by and see those of you who are dependent on Social Security deprived of the benefits you've worked so hard to earn. You will continue to receive your checks in the full amount due you." This speech had been billed as President Reagan's position on Social Security, a subject of much debate at the time.

After the speech, public opinion polls revealed that the great majority of the public believed that President Reagan had affirmed his support for Social Security and that he would not support cuts in benefits. Five days after the speech, however, an article in the *Philadelphia Inquirer* (July 31, 1981, p. 6A) quoted White House spokesperson David Gergen as saying that President Reagan's words had been "carefully chosen." What President Reagan did mean, according to Gergen, was that he was reserving the right to decide who was "dependent" on those benefits, who had "earned" them, and who, therefore, was "due" them.

During the 1992 Presidential campaign, candidate Bill Clinton promised tax cuts for the middle class. After the election President Bill Clinton backed away from the tax cut, "strongly hinting that the new tax will hit the middle class hardest." The *New York Times* (January 26, 1993, pp. A1, A20) quoted an anonymous chief political adviser as saying that during the campaign the President had built himself an escape hatch, if anyone was really listening. "Every time Clinton said 'I'm not going to raise taxes on the middle class,' he always added the phrase 'to pay for my programs.' He never, never, said just 'I will not raise taxes on the middle class.' He always said 'I will not raise middle-class taxes to pay for my programs.'"

This phrasing, according to the anonymous adviser, was a "distinction with a difference" that allows the President "the opportunity he now has" to raise taxes without breaking his campaign promise. Thus, it is through doublespeak that presidents can promise one thing and do the direct opposite, all the while claiming to keep their word.

failure *n.*

1. *incomplete success*

> ● President Jimmy Carter on the aborted raid to free the American hostages in Iran: "It has been an incomplete success."
>
> —*Quarterly Review of Doublespeak,* Oct. 1980

2. *delamination*

> ● The report on testing the Bradley armored troop carrier was heavily edited, with this note: "We may need to remove the word 'failure.' We could substitute delamination."

3. *success*

> ● Secretary of Defense Harold Brown, commenting on the failure of two tests of the Tomahawk missile, said that the tests were not failures because, "Failure in the past increases the probability of success in the future."

fire department *n.*
Bureau of Combustible and Fire Risks

> ● A no-smoking sign in Newark, New Jersey, was put up by the "Bureau of Combustible and Fire Risks." Whatever happened to the fire department?
>
> —*Quarterly Review of Doublespeak,* Oct. 1982

fresh *mod.*
previously frozen
  see also *frozen*

frozen *mod.*
1. *deep-chilled*

Question: When is a frozen chicken a "fresh" chicken? Answer: When it's a "deep-chilled" chicken. For quite a few years the U.S. Department of Agriculture has allowed poultry producers to put a "fresh" label on chickens that have been frozen hard enough to make pretty good bowling balls, frozen all the way down to 0˚F. Frank Perdue, the poultry tycoon, even ran television commercials in which he used a competitor's "fresh" chicken to hammer a nail into a board. But such chickens are not frozen, says the USDA; they are "deep chilled." That included chickens that were frozen solid and then thawed and sold as "fresh."

Since "there is little or no market for poultry that cannot be labeled or marketed as 'fresh,'" according to the National Broiler Council, the chicken dealers' trade association, the pressure is on to keep the label "fresh" on frozen chickens. After all, chickens labeled "fresh" sell for as much as $2 a pound more than chickens labeled "frozen." That works out to about $1 billion moving from consumers' pockets to the pockets of those who sell frozen chickens under a government-approved "fresh" label.

When the State of California decided that a frozen chicken is a frozen chicken and they didn't care what the USDA and the poultry dealers said, the Broiler Council sued in federal court and won, because federal rules preempt state laws. "We affirm this absurdity," wrote the court. "Congress has given federal bureaucrats the power to order that frozen chickens be labeled fresh."

But the fight against frozen "fresh" chickens continued until, in response to complaints that calling "fresh" a chicken that had once been a solid block of ice was just a little misleading, the folks at Agriculture decided to recommend a change in labels. They proposed that any chicken that has seen the low side of 28˚F should be labeled "hard-chilled." The poultry folks were not happy and mounted a big effort to get the USDA to change this radical labeling effort. While the poultry folks didn't win, they did get the USDA to change the proposed "hard chilled" to "previously frozen."

But even this change was too much for the poultry people, so they went directly to the source of all linguistic wisdom: Congress. Led by Virginia Senator John Warner, 19 Senators from the poultry-producing states in the Southeast got Congress to decide on no change in the labeling of frozen chickens. So Congress, in its wisdom, rejected the proposed change and let stand the current regulation. So you can still drive nails or go bowling with an official "fresh" chicken.

—*Time*, July 24, 1995;
New York Times, Oct. 18, 1995

2. *fresh*

  • The USDA considers processed chickens "fresh," not frozen, if they have been chilled to 28° Fahrenheit. Chickens so processed have not been frozen but "deep-chilled." —*Philadelphia Inquirer*, July 21, 1981

3. *hard-chilled*
  see also *fresh*

ghetto *n.*
1. *substandard housing*
2. *inner city*
3. *rough-and-tumble neighborhood*
4. *blighted neighborhood*

  • Miami, FL, doesn't have "slums" or "ghettos"; it has "blighted neighborhoods" or "rough-and-tumble neigh-borhoods." —*Washington Post*, Sept. 9, 1993

good rules *n.*
appropriate judgmental standards

> • The Clinton Administration doesn't propose good rules; it proposes "appropriate judgmental standards."
> —*Cincinnati Enquirer,* Dec. 20, 1992

government waste *n.*
excessive resource usage

> • The Clinton Administration's term for government waste is excessive resource usage.
> —*Cincinnati Enquirer,* Dec. 20, 1992

hazard *n.*
mitigation of risk

> • The EPA explained that instead of talking about "degree of hazard," it will talk about "degree of mitigation risk."   —*Doublespeak*

is *v.*

> • "It depends upon what the meaning of the word *is* means. If is means is and never has been, that is one thing. If it means 'there is none,' that was a completely true statement."
> —President Bill Clinton from the *Philadelphia Inquirer*
> Sept. 22, 1998

job training *n.*
lifetime learning occupational development

> • For the Clinton Administration it's not job training but "lifetime learning occupational development."
> —*Cincinnati Enquirer,* Dec. 20, 1992

The Clinton Administration invented the term "investment deficit," which is defined as the additional amount of money the federal government ought to be spending. In other words, an "investment deficit" is more deficit we should be taking on because of the existing deficit. Now follow this doublespeak carefully. The way to reduce this investment deficit is to increase the budget deficit. We need to increase the budget deficit so that we can reduce the investment deficit, a deficit most people never even knew existed, probably because it doesn't exist.

The term "investment deficit" is a classic example of doublespeak, wherein a reassuring word (investment) is coupled with a frightening word (deficit) in order to justify larger spending by government.

President Clinton seems very fond of the word "investment." For him there is very little spending and a whole lot of investing. He used "investment" as a substitute for the word "spending" in his rhetoric on economic policy, calling for "an immediate package of jobs investments of over $30 billion . . ." and additional "investments in education, technology, environmental cleanup and converting from a defense to a domestic economy."

—*Weekly Compilation of Presidential Documents,* Feb. 17, 1993; Feb. 22, 1993

lose an election *v.*
deselected

manhole *n.*
maintenance hole

overthrow a government *v.*
1. *destabilize*
2. *unconsolidate*

poison gas *n.*
inhalation hazard

> • Although experts recommended that the classification of anhydrous ammonia be changed from "non-flammable gas" to "poison gas" because of the large number of deaths and injuries caused by accidental spills, the Department of Transportation decided to change the classification to "inhalation hazard."
>
> —*San Francisco Chronicle,* Aug. 16, 1989

precondition *n.*
unilateral declaration of intent

> • Robert C. McFarlane, President Reagan's national security advisor, said that Moscow was misinterpreting Washington's position on proposed talks on space weapons. He said that the American proposal that the talks consider offensive nuclear weapons as well as space arms was not a "precondition" but a "unilateral declaration of intent."
>
> —*New York Times,* Aug. 2, 1984

propaganda *n.*
1. *overseas publicity*

> • China's leaders held a meeting on improving overseas propaganda, which China's official English language publications did not translate as a meeting on propaganda. Instead, they translated the meeting's topic—*xuanchuan* in Chinese—as "a meeting on the work of overseas publicity."
>
> —*New York Times,* Nov. 6, 1990

2. *controlled communication*

3. *domestic fallout*
4. *condition the public*

> ● A senior Clinton Administration official said they could have done more "to condition the public" to the need for a military invasion of Haiti.
>
> —*New York Times,* Sept. 15, 1994

recession *n.*

1. *period of negative economic growth*

> ● Thomas Murphy, the president of General Motors, said in an interview on the television program "Meet the Press" that the reason automobile sales were so bad is that "we are in a period of negative economic growth."
>
> —*Quarterly Review of Doublespeak,* Jan. 1981

2. *contained depression*
3. *severe adjustment process*

> ● The Bank of Japan announced a lowering of interest rates as a response to what it described as a "severe adjustment process" taking place in the economy. Even Japanese politicians don't like to use the dreaded "r" word, recession.
>
> —*New York Times,* July 27, 1992

4. *involuntary downward deployment of the workforce*
5. *meaningful downturn in aggregate output*
6. *negative economic growth*
7. *economic shortfall*
8. *period of adjustment*
9. *period of accelerated negative growth*
10. *suppression of economic activity*

11. *temporary interruption of an economic expansion*

• Among the words and phrases used by government officials in Canada to avoid the dreaded word "recession" are retrenchment, slowdown, tough times, negative growth, period of adjustment, sustainable growth that can't go on forever, pause in the economy and economic shortfall.   *—Toronto Star,* Oct. 14, 1990

reduce government regulations *v.*
create a more enabling regulatory environment

• The Clinton folk prefer to "create a more enabling regulatory environment."
—Cincinnati Enquirer, Dec. 20, 1992

In the doublespeak of President Clinton, a proposed tax on an additional 35 percent of Social Security benefits isn't a tax. Since such a tax would mean that less money would be paid out in Social Security benefits, the proposed tax became a spending cut. Similarly, the proposal to uncap the sum on which the Medicare tax is levied was also called a spending cut. In addition, the new health care plan proposed by President Clinton would have been at least partly financed by a "wage-based premium." In other words, a tax.
—New York Times, Feb. 22, 1993;
Time, May 24, 1993

slum *n.*
ghetto

spy *n.*
1. *human intelligence resource* (CIA)
2. *covert human collection resource*
3. *intelligence specialist*

You may not be able to bribe a politician, but you can buy "access to the system." During the 1996 elections, the Democratic National Committee published a brochure listing the various forms of access you could buy and how much each access cost. For $1,000 a year, you got a reception where you would have met Hillary Clinton, Tipper Gore, or a few top women administration officials. But the highest access was for those who could afford much more. At $100,000 a year you became a "Managing Trustee" of the Democratic Party, entitling you to two meals with President Clinton, two meals with Vice President Gore, participation in two "issues retreats," private meetings with administration officials when they visited your hometown, "Honored Guest Status" at the 1996 Chicago convention, and a personal staff member from the Democratic National Committee to assist you with your "personal requests." In addition, you could have traveled with Democratic Party leaders when they went on a foreign trade mission, and you got daily faxes filled with inside information. So, what did the ordinary people, the people who couldn't afford to buy access, get out of this? Said Senator Christopher Dodd, one of the people who designed this brochure, "Hopefully, good government, as Huey Long would say."

But good government is not the same as "access to the system," as those who defend this system of buying influence feebly maintain. Ron Mazzoli, a former member of Congress, observed, "People who contribute get the ear of the member [of Congress] and the ear of the staff. They have the access—and access is it. Access is power. Access is clout. That's how this thing works."

—*New York Times,* July 9, 1995;
Wall Street Journal, Sept. 7, 1995

spy satellite *n.*
technical collection source

unemployment *n.*
negative employment growth

> • Officials of the Clinton Administration don't talk about unemployment; they prefer the term "negative employment growth."
>
> —*Cincinnati Enquirer*, Dec. 20, 1992

unpopular (POLITICIAN) *mod.*
candidate lacks a positive reference output

welfare recipient *n.*
self-sufficiency participant

wiretap *n.*
conduct electronic surveillance

The NRC Lexicon

The Nuclear Regulatory Commission and the nuclear power industry have developed a whole lexicon of doublespeak that they use to downplay the dangers of nuclear power plants and nuclear accidents.

earthquake
seismic event

explosion in a nuclear power plant
energetic disassembly, energy release, rapid release of energy

fire in a nuclear power plant
rapid oxidation, incendiary event

meltdown
core disruptive accident

plutonium contamination
infiltration, migration, breach of containment, plutonium has taken up residence

reactor accident
event, unusual event, unscheduled event, incident, abnormal evolution, normal aberration, plant transient, normally expected abnormal occurrence

The NRC even uses doublespeak when counting accidents at nuclear power plants and reporting them to Congress. In one report, the NRC counted as one "abnormal occurrence" accidents at 19 different reactors. How do 19 accidents become one accident? Since the 19 different reactors all had the same design flaw, and since the NRC counts "generic" problems such as design flaws built into many different reactors as one problem, the "abnormal occurrence" caused by this design flaw was really only one accident.

9

Education

....

expel (FROM SCHOOL) *v.*
expedite progress toward alternate life pursuits

- A memorandum dated July 9, 1991, noted that for students who are not doing well academically, the university "expedites their progress toward alternate life pursuits."

    —Quarterly Review of Doublespeak, Apr. 1992

fail (IN SCHOOL) *v.*
1. *awarded a non-passing grade*
2. *deficient at a grading period*

- On the "McNeil/Lehrer Report" for October 23, 1985, Eddie Joseph, president of the Texas High School Coaches Association, said of students who get failing grades: "They're not failing; they're deficient at a grading period." A new Texas law prevents students who have "F" grades from participating in extracurricular activities.

    —Quarterly Review of Doublespeak, Apr. 1986

3. *PNA (Performance Not Acceptable)* (DOD)

> • In the Navy, one does not fail an exam; one gets a "PNA," or Performance Not Acceptable.
>
> —*Quarterly Review of Doublespeak*, Oct. 1988

hallway *n.*

1. *physical freeway*
2. *behavior-transition corridor*

home economics *n.*

1. *human resources*
2. *family studies*
3. *human ecology*

> • The University of Texas calls its former Department of Home Economics the "Department of Human Ecology."   —*Quarterly Review of Doublespeak*, Apr. 1991

learning *n.*

1. *adjusted behavior*
2. *outcomes*

> • A Colorado educational consulting firm issued a report on higher education that contains the following sentence: "Current decennial review processes required by the board should include a more explicit outcomes component."
>
> —*Quarterly Review of Doublespeak*, Oct. 1988

> • The following is one of the three major goals of the University of Minnesota Technical College at Crookston: "To adjust our curriculum to reflect student outcomes." —*Quarterly Review of Doublespeak*, Jan. 1989

Teachers are "educators" these days, or "classroom managers," or "learning facilitators" who possess effective "instructional delivery skills," which they demonstrate in "micro-teaching sessions." Teaching is called the "learning process" and learning is called "adjusted behavior." Students don't study; they spend "time on task" in their "learning environment." Students who skip school don't have to worry about the truant officer. If they live in New York, they worry about the "attendance teacher." Students don't take swimming lessons. It's "instructional swim."

Teachers rarely test students these days. Instead they "implement an evaluation program," "conduct a needs assessment" (or better yet, "implement a needs assessment strategy") or prepare an "analysis of readiness skills" using an "evaluation tool (or instrument)." At Taft Junior High School in San Diego, California, students don't pass a grade; they "articulate." When students select the subjects they want to take in the next grade, it's called "articulation." Students ride to school on a "transportation component," which is operated by a "certified adolescent transportation specialist." When teachers go on a camping trip it becomes an "outdoor education interdepartmental articulation conference." Even the coaches get in on the doublespeak when they call a stopwatch an "ascending timing device" or a "descending timing device.

"The best schools are up on all the latest theories in education. First, you should remember that the very best schools aren't schools at all but "primary or secondary educational institutions" where "empirical-rational," "normative-re-educative" or "power-coercive" strategies of learning address the "situational parameters" through a variety of "implementation approaches" taking into account "multidisciplinary methodologies" in an "ecocultural framework" as educators develop "brain-based programs" of "content-specificity." Dedicated teachers, while worried about the burden of "excessive horizontal job enlargement," will still engage in a "healthy interface" in a "dual-communication mode of highly interactive student-oriented teacher methodology" designed to promote and enhance a child's "learning style" in "life-coping skills."

Hi and Lois

Reprinted with special permission of King Features Syndicate.

SHOE/By Jeff MacNelly

library *n.*
1. *learning resource center*
2. *information center*

low test scores *n.*
negative gain in test scores

Merry Christmas *interj.*
Happy Seasonal Interlude

> • A notice to staff members in a public school district
> wished them "a happy Seasonal Interlude" during the
> Christmas and New Year holiday vacation period.
> —*Quarterly Review of Doublespeak*, Apr. 1985

off-campus housing *n.*
approved alternate living environment

> • A college requires freshmen students to live in dormitories unless they received permission to live in an "approved alternate living environment."
>
> —*Quarterly Review of Doublespeak,* Apr. 1986

physical education *n.*
1. *human kinetics*

> • At Rutgers College of Rutgers University, there is no longer a Physical Education Department; it's now called the Department of Human Kinetics.
>
> —*Quarterly Review of Doublespeak,* Jan. 1981

2. *movement science*
3. *human biodynamics*
4. *human movement*
5. *kinesiology*
6. *sport exercise science*
7. *human performance* (Foothill College, Los Altos Hills, CA)

plagiarism *n.*
improperly dependent on a source

reform school *n.*
youth development center

remedial instruction *n.*
1. *college preparatory instruction*

In 1982, the Japanese Education Ministry directed textbook publishers to "update" the accounts of Japan's invasion of China in 1931. In the new textbooks, the Japanese invasion of China became the Japanese "advance." Accounts of the slaughter of an estimated 300,000 Chinese men, women and children and the raping, looting and arson by Japanese troops during the 1937 capture of Nanjing were deleted from all textbooks. The annexation of Korea in 1910 became an "advance" of Japanese forces and the establishment of a "supervisory government," while the 1919 uprising of Koreans against the Japanese occupation forces became a "riot." Outlawing the Korean language became "education in the Japanese language" in the "updated" Japanese textbooks, while Korean civilians who were forced into work gangs for the Japanese forces were called "voluntary laborers." The last Korean king simply "resigned." The "updated" textbooks made no mention of the thousands of young Korean girls who were forcibly packed off to the front lines to serve as "wartime ladies of consolation" for Japanese troops.

When this official revision of history became known, Korean and Chinese officials protested. After much discussion, the Japanese announced some revisions in their revisions of history. The revised textbooks now refer to the "so-called Nanjing massacre," which was an episode of "mad confusion" during which innumerable soldiers and civilians were killed.

—*Newsweek,* Aug. 9, 1982; *New York Times Magazine,* Oct. 27, 1985; *New York Times,* July 10, 1986

2. *additional preparation*

- "Remedial instruction" implies that students have deficiencies that must be corrected; instead, such students require "additional preparation."   —*Doublespeak*

3. *college preparatory adult education*

> • The Omnibus Education Act of 1984 passed by the Florida state legislature changed some terminology in the Florida statutes dealing with remedial education. In place of "remedial and developmental instruction" there is now "college preparatory instruction," while "remediation" becomes "additional preparation" and "remedial courses" become "college preparatory adult education" or "college preparatory instruction."
>
> —*Florida State Statutes*, Section 240.117

4. *modified course offered for those children who achieve a deficiency*

> • A child brought home a note announcing that "there will be a modified English course offered for those children who achieve a deficiency in English."
>
> —*Quarterly Review of Doublespeak*, Apr. 1986

school desk *n.*
pupil station

standing still *mod.*
spatial anchoring

student *n.*
education user

study *v.*
to spend time on task

teacher *n.*
1. *learning facilitator*
2. *classroom manager*

teaching *n.*
learning process

test *n.*
feedback

tuition increase *n.*
fee for quality

> • Trenton State College, now called the College of New Jersey, didn't raise its tuition; it instituted a "fee for quality."   —*New York Times,* July 10, 1992

10

Sex and
the Sexes

alone *mod.*

 • "Well, again, it depends on how you define alone. . . .
There were a lot of times when we were alone, but I
never really thought we were."
                    —President Bill Clinton, Sept. 17, 1998

aural sex *n.*
inappropriate sexual banter

 • President Bill Clinton testified that "I also had occasional telephone conversations . . . that included inappropriate sexual banter."
                    —Philadelphia Inquirer, Sept. 22, 1998

birth control *n.*
1. *appropriate population policies*
2. *appropriate demographic policies*

 • Participants at the United Nations Conference on
Environment and Development in Rio de Janeiro issued
a declaration that, among other things, endorses the pro-
motion of "appropriate demographic policies," which is
the closest they could come to endorsing birth control.
                    —Time, June 1, 1992

© Tom Tomorrow

doll (FOR BOYS) *n.*

1. *action figure*

> ● Hasbro initially resisted paying import tariffs on G.I.
> Joe "dolls" because they are action figures, meant for
> boys to play with, rather than dolls, which are meant
> for girls.   *—The New Doublespeak*

2. *action toy*

> ● A Wall Street analyst pointed out that toys like G.I.
> Joe and He Man are not boys' dolls; they are action
> toys.   *—Time,* July 31, 1989

erogenous zones *n.*
enumerated areas

> ● President Bill Clinton testified about "contact . . . with the enumerated areas, if the contact is done with an intent to arouse or gratify."
> —*Philadelphia Inquirer,* Sept. 22, 1998

married *mod.*
formerly single

> ● A personal ad from a newspaper announces that a "formerly single man" seeks a single or married woman.
> —*Quarterly Review of Doublespeak,* July 1988

nonsexual relations *n.*

> ● Q. Well, the grand jury would like to know, Mr. President, why it is that you think that oral sex performed on you does not fall within the definition of sexual relations. . . . A. Because that is—if the deponent is the person who has oral sex performed on him, then the contact is . . . with the lips of another person."
> —*Philadelphia Inquirer,* Sept. 22, 1998

oral sex *n.*
inappropriate intimate contact

> ● President Bill Clinton testified that "on certain occasions" he had "inappropriate, intimate contact." "Q. Did Monica Lewinsky perform oral sex on you? A. I had intimate contact with her that was inappropriate."
> —*Philadelphia Inquirer,* Sept. 22, 1998

sex shop *n.*
intimacy salon

sexual intercourse *n.*
penile insertive behavior

> • In a statement on distributing condoms in high schools, the San Francisco Board of Education referred to "penile insertive behavior" and not sexual intercourse.   —*San Francisco Chronicle,* Dec. 3, 1992

sexual relations *n.*
1. *inappropriate relationship*

> • "Indeed I did have a relationship . . . that was not appropriate."
> —President Bill Clinton, *New York Times,* Aug. 18, 1998

2. *improper contact*

> • "Yes, we were alone from time to time . . . even when there was absolutely no improper contact occurring."—President Bill Clinton, *Philadelphia Inquirer,*
> Sept. 22, 1998

swap spouses *v.*
engage in consensual non-monogamy

11

Business and Finance

bank loans *n.*
See *unpaid loans*

bankrupt *mod.*
have a substantial negative net worth

> • First South Savings and Loan of Pine Bluff, Arkansas, announced that it has a "substantial negative net worth," which "means that it has no capital and its obligations exceed its assets." In other words, they're broke.   —*Little Rock Gazette,* Sept. 27, 1987

bankruptcy *n.*
positive restructuring

black-and-white television set *n.*
non-multicolor capability

boycott *n.*
selective buying campaign

On May 9, 1978, a National Airlines 727 airplane crashed while attempting to land at the Pensacola, Florida, airport. Three of the 52 passengers aboard the airplane were killed. As a result of the crash, National made an after-tax insurance benefit of $1.7 million, or an extra 18 cents a share dividend for its stockholders. Now, National Airlines had two problems: It did not want to talk about one of its airplanes crashing, and it had to account for the $1.7 million when it issued its annual report to its stockholders. Airplanes never crash. They may have controlled flight into terrain, or they may make unscheduled contact with the ground, but in the doublespeak of the airlines they never crash. So what was National to do?

Simple. National solved the problem by inserting a footnote in its annual report explaining that the $1.7 million income was due to "the involuntary conversion of a 727." Thus with legal and accounting jargon could National fulfill its legal obligation to acknowledge the crash of its airplane and the profit it made from the crash without once mentioning the accident or the deaths.

—*San Francisco Chronicle,*
July 19, 1978

• The National Association for the Advancement of Colored People has instituted a "selective buying campaign" (not a boycott) against Coors Beer.

—*USA Today,* Apr. 5, 1984

buy *v.*
invest in

cartel *n.*
producers' cooperative

changed *mod.*
enhanced

close (FACTORY OR BUSINESS) *v.*
1. *volume-related production schedule adjustment*

> • "General Motors Corporation today reported a volume-related production schedule adjustment at its Chevrolet–Pontiac–Canada (CPC) Group Framingham (MA) assembly plant." It closed the plant permanently and laid off over 5,000 workers.
> —*Boston Globe,* Nov. 10, 1987

2. *elimination of marginal outlets*
3. *disposition of low throughput marketing units*
4. *re-evaluation and consolidation of operations*

> • Oil companies have been forced to "re-evaluate and consolidate their operations," which has meant the "elimination of marginal outlets" and the "disposition of low throughput marketing units." Doesn't anybody fire employees, close gas stations, and cut back on expenses because there's an oil glut and because people aren't buying as much gas and oil as they once did?
> —*Quarterly Review of Doublespeak,* Aug. 1982

5. *indefinite idling*
6. *plant utilization procedure*

> • General Motors announced "a series of plant utilization procedures," which means they're closing a bunch of plants.   —*Detroit News,* Dec. 4, 1992

Coke machine (VENDING MACHINE) *n.*
immediate consumption channel

Trying to find any meaning in Alan Greenspan's language is like the ancient Greeks and Romans trying to find meaning in the flight of birds, the pattern of lightning in the sky or in the entrails of a sacrificed animal.

Let's look at what Mr. Greenspan says about interest rates. "Our monetary policy strategy must continue to rest on ongoing assessments of the totality of incoming information and appraisals of the probable outcomes and risks associated with alternative policies."

Well, then, how about the effects of an interest rate increase on the bond market? "When the Federal Reserve tightens reserve market conditions, it is not surprising to see some upward movement in long-term rates as an aspect of the process that counters the imbalances tending to surface in the expansionary phase of the business cycle."

Let's go back to interest rates. Any chance the Federal Reserve might increase them? "Our long-run strategy implies that the Federal Reserve must take care not to overstay an accommodative stance as the headwinds abate."

How about monetary policy? "I think where the confusion arises is the fact that you cannot view monetary policy as a sort of simple issue of, if the most probable outcome is coming out of this soft patch into moderate growth with low inflation, which I think is the most probable outcome, that is not the same statement as saying that you therefore, in the process of implementing monetary policy or formulating it, I should say, completely disregard what the upsides and downsides of a potential outcome may be."

The next time Alan Greenspan makes a solemn pronouncement, just remember what he said in 1988: "I guess I should warn you, if I turn out to be particularly clear, you've probably misunderstood what I've said."

—*Business Week,* Mar. 14, 1994;
New York Times, July 14, 1996;
Fortune, Aug. 15, 1988

cut the budget *v.*
manage the budget

decline (IN PROFITS) *n.*
significant adverse financial effect

deregulation (OF AN INDUSTRY) *n.*
destructive competition

> • Milk sales in the State of New York are governed by
> a series of state laws and regulations that restrict who
> can sell milk in each county. In New York City and its
> immediate suburbs, the number of licensees is restricted
> to prevent what state officials call "destructive compe-
> tition." Prices for milk in New York City are substan-
> tially higher than in surrounding areas.
> —*New York Times*, Feb. 7, 1986

discount *mod.*
1. *value-oriented*

> • Franklin Mills, a new shopping center under con-
> struction in Philadelphia, will be "value-oriented," which
> means it will be a discount mall. However, developers
> of the mall insist that the stores will have an "upscale"
> flair. Some of us might say that they're going to sell
> inexpensive goods in nice stores.
> —*Philadelphia Daily News*, May 12, 1987

2. *off-price*

door *n.*
entry system

• Menards Builders Supply, which is a lumberyard, advertises "entry systems"–also known as doors.

–*Quarterly Review of Doublespeak,* Jan. 1990

electric bill *n.*
energy document

employee theft *n.*
inventory shrinkage

explosion *n.*
uncontained engine failure

• The engine on United flight 232 didn't explode; the engine just came apart in a catastrophic loss known in the industry as an "uncontained engine failure."

–*New York Times,* July 22, 1989

failed *mod.*
sub-optimal

fan *n.*
1. *air-moving device*
2. *high-velocity multipurpose air circulator*

• The Lakewood Engineering & Manufacturing Co. of Chicago doesn't make electric fans; they make "high-velocity multipurpose air circulators."

–*Philadelphia Inquirer,* May 27, 1992

farmer's market *n.*
unique retail biosphere

fee *n.*

1. *user charge*

● In April 1987, Budget Director James Miller declared that a new $1-per-ticket fee for airline and cruise tickets into and out of the U.S. was a "user charge."
—*Wall Street Journal,* Jan. 9,1987

2. *voluntary contribution*

fire drill *n.*

1. *relocation drill*
2. *evacuation drill*

● At one company, fire drills are "relocation drills" (formerly known as evacuation drills).
—*Quarterly Review of Doublespeak,* Jan. 1985

foot (12 INCHES) *n.*
8 inches

● According to the National Hot Dog and Sausage Council rules, the term "foot long" may be applied to any frankfurter that is longer than 8 inches.

for our convenience *mod.*
for your convenience

● As a subway train was pulling into a Baltimore station, an announcement on the public address system said, "Please board only those cars with lights on and doors open, for your convenience." One passenger noted, "Doors open for our convenience? I had a momentary vision of a platform full of Incredible Hulks who would simply knock down those doors, if need be—however inconvenient."
—*Quarterly Review of Doublespeak,* Apr. 1985

Think running a business means making a good product and selling it? Not at all. These days corporations talk about "globalization," "competitive dynamics," "re-equitizing," "empowerment," and "paradigm shifts." To do all this they need a "corporate vision," which is the "organizational designs and operating processes that reinforce the behaviors necessary for successful execution of our particular strategies, including operating in an entrepreneurial, empowered, accountable, team-oriented, functionally integrated, non-bureaucratic way, where . . . managers communicate, motivate, facilitate, integrate and develop rather than direct and do."

If that vision leads to a loss of business, corporations don't say they lost money. They just report "negative cash flow," "deficit enhancement," "net profit revenue deficiencies" or "negative contributions to profits."

Corporations do not have a problem with employees offering bribes or taking kickbacks. They simply call them "rebates" or "fees for product testing."

No one gets fired these days, and no one gets laid off. Those high enough in the corporate pecking order "resign for personal reasons." People are never unemployed; they're just in an "orderly transition between career changes." But even those far below the lofty heights of corporate power are not fired or laid off. During these days of "cost rationalization," "reengineering," "restructuring," and "downsizing," companies fire or lay off workers many different ways.

Companies make "workforce adjustments" or "census reductions" or institute a program of "negative employee retention." Corporations offer workers "vocational relocation," "career assignment and relocation," a "career-change opportunity," or "voluntary termination." Workers are "dehired," "deselected," "selected out," "repositioned," "surplused," "right-sized," "correct sized," "excessed," or "uninstalled." Some companies "initiate operations improvements," "assign candidates to a mobility pool," "implement a skills mix adjustments," or "eliminate redundancies in the human resources area."

One company denied it was laying

off 500 people. "We don't characterize it as a layoff," said the corporate spin doctor. "We're managing our staff resources. Sometimes you manage them up, and sometimes you manage them down."

Firing workers is such big business that there are companies whose business is helping other companies fire workers by providing "termination and outplacement consulting" for corporations involved in "reduction activities." But don't worry—for those who are "managed down," the "Outplacement Consultant" will help them with "re-employment engineering."

haunted *mod.*
psychologically impacted

> • The real estate profession calls houses where murder or suicides have occurred, or where ghosts supposedly dwell, "psychologically impacted."
> —*Wall Street Journal,* Oct. 31, 1991

interest rate *n.*
service rate

> • According to the American Banking Association, "Some say the interest rate [on bank credit cards] is too high. Don't call it an interest rate. Call it a service rate." —*Common Cause Magazine,* Mar.–Apr. 1986

irregular *mod.*
1. *practically perfect*

2. *slightly imperfect*

> • In the hosiery business, there are two principal clas-
> sifications of quality: first-quality and irregulars. But
> now two of the largest manufacturers have changed
> the classification of their irregulars, with one calling
> them "slightly imperfect" and the other calling them
> "practically perfect."
>
> —*Quarterly Review of Doublespeak,* Oct. 1988

janitorial services *n.*
environmental services

> • At Madison General Hospital in Madison, Wiscon-
> sin, janitorial services are performed by the staff of
> "environmental services."
>
> —*Quarterly Review of Doublespeak,* Apr. 1984

junk *n.*
predismantled, previously owned parts

> • It's no longer auto junkyards, or even junk. Now
> it's "auto dismantlers and recyclers" who sell "predis-
> mantled, previously owned parts."
>
> —*Time,* May 16, 1983

junk bonds *n.*
1. *distressed securities*
2. *below investment grade securities*

junkyard *n.*
1. *resource development park*
2. *reutilization marketing yard*

"On Wall Street today, the stock market was down.
Analysts say this was because more people wanted to
sell stocks than buy them."

● The federal government calls a junkyard a "reutilization marketing yard." Does that mean that junkyard dogs are really "reutilization marketing yard
dogs?"   —*Quarterly Review of Doublespeak,* Oct. 1989

kickback *n.*
See *bribe*

leftovers *n.*
outstanding vintage cuisine

linoleum *n.*
resilient vinyl flooring

> • Once upon a time, people bought linoleum to cover their floors. Now they buy "resilient vinyl flooring."
> —*Advertising Age,* June 13, 1988

lose money *v.*
1. *net profit revenue deficiencies*
2. *negative contributions to profits*
3. *negatively impact profitability*
4. *negative gross profit*

low sales *n.*
reduced demand for product

mistake *n.*
variance

> • Pacific Bell has a "variance elimination program," which is designed to "help employees avoid variances on initial service orders" and which has resulted in a 20 percent drop in "service order variances." In other words, the company is working to reduce the number of mistakes made by employees.
> —*Quarterly Review of Doublespeak,* Oct. 1988

out of stock *mod.*
ship period violation

> • Usually, when a company does not ship an item that was ordered, it will note that the item is "out of stock" or "discontinued" or use a similar phrase. Bristol-Meyers uses the phrase "ship period violation" on its invoices. —*Quarterly Review of Doublespeak,* Apr. 1985

The next time you want to buy some hot dogs, sausage, luncheon meat, scrapple or canned spaghetti with meat sauce you might want to read the list of ingredients on the label very carefully. Does the list of ingredients include "Mechanically Separated Meat?" MSM (as it's called in the food trade) is the salvaged remnants of slaughtered animals, including bones, connecting tissue and attached scraps of meat, passed through a grinder and then pressed through sieves until most of the bone is filtered out. (Some pieces of ground bone are always left in the mixture, but then no process is perfect.)

Until 1982 this stuff was called "salvaged meat," but for some reason it just wasn't selling, probably because manufacturers were required to label the amount of "powdered bone" the mixture contained. But then the U.S. Department of Agriculture came to the rescue. Suddenly "salvaged meat" became "Mechanically Separated Meat," and the list of ingredients on a label would no longer have to include "ground bone" as an ingredient. All that would have to be listed on the label was "Mechanically Separated Meat" and the amount of "calcium" in the average serving.

But the meat processing industry still wasn't happy. In 1988 Bob Evans Farms Inc., the Odom Sausage Company, the Sara Lee Corporation and Owen Country Sausage Inc. petitioned the Department of Agriculture to allow hot dogs and other products to contain up to 10 percent MSM without listing it as an ingredient. Now, even the innocuous phrase "Mechanically Separated Meat" is no longer on the label. But don't worry; the amount of "calcium" per serving is still listed, because the ground bone is still there.

—*Atlanta Journal and Constitution,* Sept. 14, 1988; *New York Times,* Sept. 13, 1988; *Seattle Times,* Oct. 1, 1988

overbooking *mod.*

1. *space planning*
2. *capacity management*
3. *revenue control*

plunger *n.*
hydro blast force cup

> • An advertisement labeled that good old plumber's helper, the plunger, a "hydro blast force cup."
>
> —*Chicago Tribune,* Mar. 4, 1984

price decrease *n.*
value pricing

price increase *n.*

1. *price enhancement*

> • A Department of Agriculture study admitted that the practice of issuing marketing orders that strictly control the amounts of produce that farmers may sell to processors causes "price enhancement."
>
> —*Philadelphia Inquirer,* July 20, 1981

2. *upward adjustment*
3. *economic adjustment*
4. *price realignment*

profit *n.*

1. *negative deficit*

> • An official at the Wharton School of Business of the University of Pennsylvania stated that the Wharton Executive Education Program does not make a profit but instead runs a "negative deficit."
>
> —*Philadelphia Magazine,* Nov. 1976

2. *revenue excesses*

3. *positive budget variance*

> • For the American Trucking Association, it's not a profit but a "positive budget variance."
>> –*Quarterly Review of Doublespeak,* Apr. 1991

4. *revenue positive*

quota *n.*

1. *materiality of adjustment in relation to assigned workloads*

2. *minimum expectations*

3. *production level*

recall a defective product *v.*

initiate a pro-active action

recession *n.*

1. *period of negative economic growth*

> • In an interview on the television program "Meet the Press, Thomas Murphy, the president of General Motors, said that the reason automobile sales were so bad is that "we are in a period of negative economic growth." –*Quarterly Review of Doublespeak,* Jan. 1981

refreshment stand *n.*

patron assistance center

> • The Strand movie theater in Madison, Wisconsin, has a Patron Assistance Center where customers can buy soda, popcorn, candy and all those things usually sold at the refreshment stand in movie theaters.
>> –*Quarterly Review of Doublespeak,* Oct. 1984

reservations (AT A RESTAURANT) *n.*
call-ahead seating

robbery of a bank OR **ATM** *n.*
1. *authorized transaction*

> • When a bank customer handed over his automatic teller machine card and access code at gunpoint, the robber's five-hundred-dollar withdrawal was an "authorized transaction" according to Texas Federal Savings and Loan. A letter to the customer stated that "Texas Federal has established a policy to consider a robbery of an ATM to be an authorized transaction."
> —*Austin* (TX) *American-Statesman,* May 23, 1984

2. *unauthorized transaction*
3. *unauthorized withdrawal*

> • A bank holdup was listed as an "unauthorized withdrawal" on the bank's books.
> —*Reader's Digest,* Sept. 1986

sale *n.*
deaccession

> • Harvard's Fogg Art Museum has decided to "deaccession" some works of art.
> —*New York Times,* Jan. 30, 1982

second mortgage *n.*
non-owner-occupied equity recovery

> • An advertisement did not say that the mortgage company offered second mortgages on rental property; instead, it offered "non-owner-occupied equity recovery." —*Dallas Morning News,* Jan. 10, 1988

sell (STOCK) *v.*
de-accumulate

sleeping *n.*
passive travel

> • A Boston law firm billed the LTV Corporation for
> "passive travel," which is the time lawyers spend sleep-
> ing in their first-class airplane seats as they fly to an
> appointment at LTV.
> —*Conservative Chronicle,* Jan. 15, 1992

smelter *n.*
onward processing unit

> • Due to public opposition to the presence and use of
> smelters, some mining companies refer to them as
> "onward processing units."
> —*Quarterly Review of Doublespeak,* July 1988

spend *v.*
invest in

stock market crash *n.*
fourth-quarter equity retreat

> • A stockbroker called the October 1987 stock market
> crash a "fourth-quarter equity retreat."
> —*Quarterly Review of Doublespeak,* Apr. 1988

strike *n.*
volume variance from plan

tract houses *n.*
production houses

trailer park *n.*
manufactured home facility

travel agency *n.*
destination management organization

unpaid loans *n.*
1. *nonperforming assets*

> • Why are so many banks in New England having trouble? Because of a "real estate correction" that has produced "nonperforming assets" for the banks.
> —*Philadelphia Inquirer,* Oct. 28, 1989

> • John Kenneth Galbraith notes that in past times, loans that were not paid were in default. Now, however, such loans are "rolled over. Or rescheduled. Or they become problem loans. Or, best of all, they are nonperforming assets."
> —*New York Times,* May 26, 1985

2. *nonperforming credits*

> • Continental Illinois Corporation reported that its "nonperforming credits" increased 44 percent in the fourth quarter to $653 million.
> —*Wall Street Journal,* Feb. 16, 1982

used *mod.*
1. *owner pretested*
2. *pre-owned*

- When is a used wristwatch not a used wristwatch? When it's a "pre-owned vintage watch classic" that is "an estate-quality timepiece" from "Tourneau's second-time-around collection."

  —*New York Times Magazine,* Oct. 2, 1988

3. *experienced*
4. *previewed*
5. *pre-enjoyed*
6. *pre-existing*
7. *renewed*

- The latest way to say "used car" is "renewed car."

  —*Quarterly Review of Doublespeak,* July 1988

8. *previously enjoyed.*

- Did you know that a "previously enjoyed" television set is a used television set offered for sale by a company that rents television sets?

  —*Quarterly Review of Doublespeak,* Jan. 1989

used refrigerator *n.*
renewed appliance

- Copland's Appliance Store in Milwaukee, Wisconsin, advertised a "renewed appliance" sale.

  —*Quarterly Review of Doublespeak,* Jan. 1990

waiting room *n.*
customer convenience area

washing machine *n.*
laundry system

wastepaper business *n.*
secondary fiber business

> • "We're not a wastepaper business. We're a secondary fiber business," said the president of the company. To city officials, however, "a secondary fiber business is a wastepaper business is a junkyard."
>
> —*Philadelphia Inquirer*, Dec. 17, 1983

waterproof *mod.*
have negative vulnerability to water entry

window *n.*
environmentally operable panel

> • The apartment building had many features, according to the architect's brochure. Among them were "environmentally operable panels," or windows that could be opened.
>
> —*Quarterly Review of Doublespeak*, July 1988

worst *mod.*
least best

> • United Parcel Service prefers to refer to its "worst" drivers as its "least best."
>
> —*Quarterly Review of Doublespeak*, Jan. 1984

12

Job Titles

bank teller *n.*
1. *financial services specialist*
2. *teller services representative*

beautician *n.*
1. *esthetician*
2. *estheticienne*

> • The Lancome Institute de Beaute is looking for an "estheticienne." Or in simpler terms, the beauty shop is looking for a beautician.
> —*Columbus* (OH) *Dispatch*, July 24, 1988

bellhop *n.*
guest service attendant

> • Westin Hotels in San Francisco is advertising for the position of Guest Service Attendant, or bellhop.
> —*Quarterly Review of Doublespeak*, Jan. 1990

bill collector *n.*
portfolio administrator

● A company advertised in the Help Wanted section for a "portfolio administrator." The job entails working in the "asset management division."

—Philadelphia Inquirer, n.d.

bodyguard *n.*
executive protection people

● No one hires bodyguards these days; now they hire a "personal protection specialist" or "protective people" from an "executive protection agency."

—Insight, Apr. 18, 1988

bus boy *n.*
1. *dining room assistant*
2. *assistant food server*

car salesperson *n.*
.1. *transportation investment consultant*
2. *purchase adviser of previously distinguished automobiles*

cashier *n.*
customer service representative

checkout clerk *n.*
See *grocery store checkout clerk*

clergy *n.*
members of the Human Ecology Department

● At Madison General Hospital in Madison, Wisconsin, members of the clergy who are on staff belong to the Human Ecology Department.

—Quarterly Review of Doublespeak, Apr. 1984

cook *n.*
subsistence specialist

> • The Coast Guard calls her husband a "subsistence specialist." She calls him a cook.
> —*Santa Clara* (CA) *News-Press,* Aug. 29, 1993

cowboy *n.*
mobile mountain range technician

doorman *n.*
access controller

elevator operator *n.*
member of the vertical transportation corps

> • The people at Hahnemann Hospital in Philadelphia wearing the insignia of the "Vertical Transportation Corps" are the elevator operators."
> —*Philadelphia Inquirer Today Magazine,* Nov. 28, 1976

exterminator *n.*
1. *senior sanitarian*
2. *one skilled in deroaching techniques*

THE WIZARD OF ID   by Brant parker and Johnny hart

By permission of Johnny Hart and Creators Syndicate, Inc.

• An environmental paper on Camden County, New Jersey, ran an article by Robert Lentine, who was identified as "Senior Sanitarian." In his article, Mr. Lentine discussed "deroaching techniques."

—*The Environmental Voice,* Apr. 1985

fire inspector *n.*
combustibles inspector

• The New Jersey Department of Civil Service changed the title of an employee from "fire inspector" to "Combustibles Inspector." A little later, he became a "Combustibles Inspector/Fire Protection Inspector." Finally he was notified that his correct title was "Fire Prevention Specialist/Fire Protection Inspector." "All of these changes and I'm still doing the same job," the employee noted.

—*Quarterly Review of Doublespeak,* July 1988

gardener *n.*
manager of vegetarian maintenance

grocer *n.*
nutritional therapist provision provider

grocery store checkout clerk *n.*
part-time career associate scanning professional

• Wegmans Food Markets in Rochester, New York, advertises for "part-time career associate scanning professionals."   —*Wall Street Journal,* June 11, 1985

janitor *n.*
1. *environmental technician*

- Want a job? How about the exciting career of "environmental technician," or janitor, as it used to be called?   —*Quarterly Review of Doublespeak,* Oct. 1988

2. *service partner*
3. *environment superintendent*
4. *environmental hygienist*

- To some, a janitor is really an "environmental hygienist."   —*College English,* Mar. 1988

5. *entropy control engineer*

- Janitors are now called "entropy control engineers."
—*Quarterly Review of Doublespeak,* Apr. 1988

6. *particulate matter remover*

- In reviewing questionnaires from prospective jurors, a judge learned that one of them was employed as a "particulate matter remover." The judge later learned the juror was a janitor.
—*Quarterly Review of Doublespeak,* July 1988

junk dealer *n.*
automobile dismantler and recycler

lineman *n.*
outside aerial technician

loan office *n.*
fulfillment office

- For the return addresses on their envelopes, credit companies do not say credit bureaus or loan offices but "fulfillment offices."
—*Quarterly Review of Doublespeak,* Apr. 1988

lobbyist *n.*
government affairs specialist

manicurist *n.*
nail technician

> • A classified want ad was listed for a "nail technician," or what used to be known as a manicurist.
> —*Quarterly Review of Doublespeak,* Apr. 1985

newspaper delivery person *n.*
media courier

> • A newspaper delivery boy insisted on being called a "media courier."   —*Reader's Digest,* Sept. 1986

nurse *n.*
patient care specialist

part-time worker *n.*
1. *just-in-time employee*
2. *peripheral*

> • IBM calls the temporary workers it hires "the peripherals."   —*Time,* Mar. 29, 1993

3. *occasional faculty*

> • The Department of Political Science at the University of Texas doesn't hire part-time or temporary teachers—it hires "occasional faculty."
> —*Star Telegram* (Fort Worth, TX), Apr. 25, 1993

peasant *n.*
impoverished agricultural worker

From the comic strip "Warped," by Mike Cavna. Reprinted by permission of Lew Little Enterprise, Inc.

pizza delivery person *n.*
delivery ambassador

plumber *n.*
drain surgeon

police officer *n.*
protective service worker

polygraph examiner *n.*
forensic psychophysiologist

> • The Defense Department plans to scrap the term
> "polygraph examiner" and replace it with "forensic
> psychophysiologist," who will administer not a lie
> detector test but a "psychophysiological detection of
> deception test."   —*Science*, Jan. 29, 1993

prostitute *n.*
1. *girl who sells her smile* (China)
2. *casual female companion*

3. *lady who takes tips*
4. *sex industry worker*

> • A newspaper article calls prostitutes "sex industry workers."
> —*Quarterly Review of Doublespeak,* July 1988

5. *priestess of love*

> • The Russian government has for years maintained that prostitution had been wiped out, so there are no legal regulations against it. While not admitting that there might be prostitution, the government has acknowledged that there are "priestesses of love," "night stalkers," "ladies of easy virtue" and "ladies who take tips" walking the streets of Moscow and other cities.   —*Philadelphia Inquirer,* Oct. 26, 1986

6. *sex care provider*

> • They're not prostitutes; they're "sex care providers"— at least according to a 1991 PBS broadcast about AIDS.
> —*Quarterly Review of Doublespeak,* Oct. 1991

7. *comfort girl* (Japan)

prostitution *n.*
1. *compensated dating*
2. *sexual surrogacy*

> • The state calls it prostitution. We call it sexual surrogacy," said the Fort Lauderdale, Florida, attorney.
> —*Toronto Sun,* Sept. 6, 1991

real estate agent *n.*
1. *registered relocation specialist*
2. *certified residential sales counselor*

repairman. *n.*
service technician

salesperson *n.*
1. *advisory market representative*

> ● At IBM the official term for salesperson is "advisory market representative."
> —*Journal Times* (Racine, WI), May 29, 1981

2. *territory manager*

> ● The salespeople of a hospital bed supply company are called "territory managers."
> —*Quarterly Review of Doublespeak*, Apr. 1988

3. *marketing consultant*
4. *purchase advisor*
5. *executive snack route consultant*
6. *leasing consultant*
7. *account executive*

secretary *n.*
1. *executive assistant*
2. *office automation specialist*

> ● "We have high school guidance counselors out here periodically for lunch, and they say, 'Never use the word secretary. Girls don't want to be secretaries,'" says Virginia Tanner, public relations director at Villa Julie College. "So we're trying to make the transition by advertising 'executive assistants' and 'office automation specialists.'"
> —*Baltimore Sun/Evening Sun*, May 21, 1985

3. *administrative assistant*

> • The ad for an Administrative Assistant listed job responsibilities as "fulfillment of marketing materials to customers and vendors" and then "coordination of shipments to trade shows and conferences," both of which mean "pack it and ship it."
>
> —*San Francisco Examiner & Chronicle*, Feb. 28, 1993

security guard *n.*

1. *security hosts*

> • At Expo 86 in Vancouver, Canada, the security police were called "security hosts."
>
> —*Monday Magazine* (Victoria, Canada),
> Mar. 27–Apr. 2, 1986

2. *loss prevention specialist*

> • Want a job? Consider the exciting field of "Loss Prevention Specialist," that is, unarmed guard at a department store.
>
> —*Richmond* (VA) *Times Dispatch*, Jan. 10, 1988

3. *night entry supervisor*

> • When the ad for a security guard for the night shift didn't attract enough applications, the company advertised for a "night entry supervisor" and got a lot of inquiries—only a few of whom asked what the title meant.
>
> —*Quarterly Review of Doublespeak*, July 1988

sewer commissioner *n.*

wastewater manager

• In one American town, they no longer have a sewer commissioner; they have a wastewater manager.
    —*Quarterly Review of Doublespeak,* Apr. 1988

stockbroker *n.*
1. *registered representative*
2. *portfolio manager*

store clerk *n.*
sales associate

supply clerk *n.*
technician coordinator

telephone line worker *n.*
See *lineman*

temporary worker *n.*
See *part-time worker*

travel agent *n.*
destination manager or *advisor*

undertaker *n.*
grief therapist

used car salesperson *n.*
purchase advisor of previously distinguished automobiles

waiter *n.*
1. *food and beverage consultant*
2. *table person*
3. *waitron*

> • According to the Random House Webster's College Dictionary, a "waitron" is "a person of either sex who waits on tables."

4. *guest service attendant* (Sizzler Steak, Seafood & Salad restaurant, Lompoc, CA)

window cleaner *n.*
fenestration engineer

writer *n.*
1. *content provider*
2. *language therapist*

13

Recreation
(Sports and Leisure)

bar *n.*
age-controlled environment

casino *n.*
multidimensional gaming with an entertainment complex

> ● Proponents of legalized gambling didn't want to use the word "casino" because it's "sort of a tough word. We're using 'multidimensional gaming with an entertainment complex.'"
>
> —*Cincinnati Enquirer*, Sept. 5, 1993

gambling *n.*
1. *gaming*
2. *applied statistics*
3. *wagering*

happy hour *n.*
attitude adjustment period

Hagar the Horrible

THAT'S NOTHING BUT *SLOTHFULNESS!*

IF I WERE RICH THEY'D CALL IT *LEISURE!*

DIK BROWNE

10-21

Reprinted with special permission of King Features Syndicate.

horse racing *n.*
large, agriculturally based industry

movie *n.*
entertainment software unit

nudism *n.*
clothing-optional recreation

> • Nudists like to say that they engage in "clothing-optional recreation." —*Chicago Tribune*, Jan. 22, 1990

slot machine *n.*
video gaming device

sports *n.*
movement experiences

swim *n.*

primary recreational contact

> • The Environmental Protection Agency announced
> that pollution control efforts had been so effective that
> parts of the Delaware River in Philadelphia are now
> suitable for "primary recreational contact." That means
> you can swim in some sections of the river as long as
> you dodge all the boats.
>
> —*KYW Radio* (Philadelphia), Nov. 1, 1987

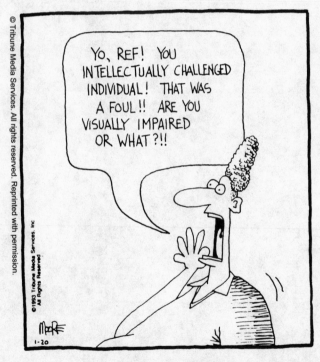

Politically correct heckling

swimming pool *n.*

aquatic therapy department

> • When the school board refused to approve funds for a swimming pool, a school principal submitted a proposal for an "Aquatic Therapy Department" for handicapped children.
>
> —*Quarterly Review of Doublespeak,* Oct. 1984

video games *n.*

dedicated entertainment hardware

14

Communication

advertisement *n.*
See *commercial*

ask for something *v.*
articulate your desires

beat up *v.*
engage in nonverbal persuasion

bossy *mod.*
exhibiting leadership charisma

> • The mother of a two-year-old who was attending a play group was told that her daughter had "leadership charisma." It meant her daughter was bossy.
> —*Quarterly Review of Doublespeak,* Oct. 1989

bug (IN A COMPUTER PROGRAM) *n.*
1. *undocumented program feature*

> • The next time you have problems running a program on your computer, just remember that there are no mistakes or flaws in a computer program, just "undocumented program features."
>
> —*Quarterly Review of Doublespeak,* Apr. 1988

2. *design side effect*
3. *undocumented behavior*

calendar *n.*

personal manual database

> • It's not a calendar. It's a "personal manual database."
> —*Better Homes and Gardens,* Jan. 1988

censor *n.*

Program Practices Department (CBS)

> • The name Program Practices Department at CBS is "the network euphemism for censor."
> —*New York Times Magazine,* Dec. 14, 1975

censor *v.*

1. *sanitize*
2. *weed*

© Tribune Media Services. All rights reserved. Reprinted with permission.

The 1990 Children's Television Act was supposed to raise the standards of television programs for children by requiring television stations to "serve the educational and informational needs of children." Stations must also provide documentation of how they are meeting this requirement when they file to renew their licenses with the FCC. To see just how well television stations were complying with this new law, the Center for Media Education in Takoma Park, Maryland, examined a bunch of the renewal forms that stations had filed. According to their own statements in these filings, this is how broadcasters are fulfilling their obligations under the new law.

Station WGNO of New Orleans said that Bucky O'Hare, a rabbit in space who fights alien toads with guns and lasers, is "educational and informational" because "issues of social consciousness and responsibility are central themes of the program." WGNO also claimed that reruns of "Leave It to Beaver" were educational.

Other stations claimed such programs as "The Jetsons," "The Flintstones," "G.I. Joe," "Superboy" and "Super Mario Brothers" contain "issues of social consciousness and responsibilities" and show the value of "communication and trust." One station cited "Chip 'n Dale Rescue Rangers" in which "the Rescue Rangers stop Cheddarhead Charlie from an evil plot. The rewards of team efforts are the focus in this episode." Other stations claimed that episodes of the "Teenage Mutant Ninja Turtles" teach about nutrition and physical fitness, while an episode of "Yo, Yogi!" in which the hero defeats a bank-robbing cockroach promotes the value of "using his head rather than his muscles." Newsweek magazine called these characterizations "imaginative" and "shameless flimflam."

—*Newsweek,* Nov. 30, 1993;
New York Times, Mar. 4, 1993; Mar. 8, 1993; Sept. 30, 1993; Oct. 4, 1993

censorship *n.*

1. *limitation on what newspapers can report*

> • Louis Nel, Deputy Minister for Information of
> South Africa, said, "To me, censorship means that every
> report must be approved before it can be published.
> We do not have censorship. What we have is a limita-
> tion on what newspapers can report."
>
> —*New York Times,* June 26, 1986

2. *administrative control*
3. *weeding books*
4. *security review*

> • During the Gulf War, news was subject to "security
> review," rather than censorship.
>
> —*The New Doublespeak*

clock *n.*

personal analog temporal displacement monitor

> • You can now own "E.W.'s personal analog temporal
> displacement monitor" for only $14.95. That is, if you
> want to pay that much for a clock.
>
> —*E.W.'s Computer Almanac, Special Edition,* Fall 1987

commercial *n.*

1. *value-added entertainment*
2. *enhanced underwriting acknowledgment* or *credits* or *corporate identity* (PBS)

> • When public television station WNET/13 in New
> York City began airing commercials, it called them
> "enhanced underwriting credits."
>
> —*Broadcast Announcements,* May 1983

3. *value minutes*

PBS may have once been commercial-free, but with budget cuts money had to be found somewhere, and what better source than advertising? Of course PBS had a slight problem, because by law it is non-commercial and not allowed to accept commercial advertising. So the Public Broadcasting System does not run commercials. It does, however, offer "enhanced underwriter acknowledgments."

Such "acknowledgments" include "value-neutral descriptions of a product line or service" and corporate logos or slogans that "identify and do not promote." Such "enhanced underwriting" is designed to attract "additional business support." While publicly maintaining that such "acknowledgments" are not commercials, officials at Public Broadcasting Marketing, a company that represents public radio and television stations, promote the "sales potential" of public television's children programming to corporations.

In a letter to Advertising Age, the president of PBM pointed out that "through Public Broadcasting Marketing, corporations can place messages adjacent to 'Sesame Street,' 'Mr. Rogers,' 'Shining Time Station' and 'Barney,' tapping the sales potential of these acclaimed programs. More and more corporations recognize PBM's unique, high-impact environment."

According to the Communications Act of 1934, these "enhanced underwriter acknowledgments" may well be illegal. This Act specifically forbids noncommercial stations from accepting compensation for broadcasting messages that "promote any service, facility or product offered by any person who is engaged in such offering for profit." But with doubles-peak PBS has maneuvered around this little legal restriction and is reaping the benefits of running ads that aren't ads.

You might think that running ads on public television and calling them "enhanced underwriter acknowledgments" isn't such a big deal, but it is. The effect of public television's dependency on advertising is to decide which programs go on the air and which don't. As Michael Fields, station manager of Pittsburgh public television station WQEX bluntly explained as he canceled three programs: "We can't afford to keep shows on the air that the business community doesn't want to support."

—*EXTRA!*, Sept./Oct. 1993

Beetle Bailey

Reprinted with special permission of King Features Syndicate.

4. *important message*
5. *advertising positioning*

fight *n.*
1. *physical altercation*
2. *socially motivated altercation*
3. *nonverbal conversation*

fight *v.*
hold a nonverbal conversation

greeting card *n.*
social expression product

> • So you thought that Hallmark made greeting cards?
> Not these days. Hallmark, you see, makes "social expres-
> sion" products.   —*New York Times,* July 14, 1985

handwriting *n.*
grapho-motor representation

- While at a teacher's convention, a teacher was confused by "grapho-motor representation" until someone explained that it means handwriting.

  –Quarterly Review of Doublespeak, July 1988

ink *n.*

writing fluid

- A customer asked for a bottle of ink, only to have the mystified clerk finally figure out that she wanted "writing fluid."

  –Quarterly Review of Doublespeak, July 1988

Calvin and Hobbes by Bill Watterson

liar *n.*
one who suffers from fictitious order syndrome

lie *n.*
1. *political credibility problem*
2. *terminological inexactitude*
3. *reality augmentation*

> • Lies told by politicians are sometimes called "reality augmentation." —*The New Doublespeak*

4. *counterfactual proposition*
5. *categorical inaccuracy*
6. *strategic misrepresentation*

> • Hiding facts, bluffing or lying during business negotiations is really "strategic misrepresentation," according to the Harvard Business School. —*Doublespeak*

7. *inoperative statement*
8. *factually flexible*

> • According to an editorial, Senator Robert Packwood of Oregon didn't lie during his re-election campaign when he denied there was a press investigation into allegations against him of sexual harassment. He was just being "factually flexible in the heat of a campaign." —*Wall Street Journal,* May 14, 1993

9. *perception management program*
10. *inaccurate statement*
11. *incomplete statement*
12. *unreliable statement*
13. *disinformation*
14. *creative license*
15. *plausible deniability*

16. *benign exaggeration*
17. *credibility gap*

> ● In an article entitled "Vietnam's Tragedy in Four Acts," Henry Kissinger states, "It was fairly simple to construct the vaunted credibility gap by reiterating the difference between government statements and what in fact happened. A fairer analysis would have sought to determine what was due to genuine confusion and what was actual misrepresentation."
>
> —*Sunday Times* (London), Apr. 14, 1985

18. *modified limited hangout*
19. *technically correct but specifically evasive*

> ● After contradicting his earlier sworn testimony, the CIA agent defended his earlier answers as "technically correct but specifically evasive."
>
> —*Philadelphia Inquirer*, Aug. 26, 1987

lie *v.*

1. *misspeak*
2. *mislead*
3. *keep cover*

> ● "The whole question of lying to Congress—you could call it a lie, but for us that's keeping cover," said the CIA agent [David Whipple].
>
> —*Philadelphia Inquirer*, Sept. 7, 1991

4. *give a false answer*
5. *be factually flexible*
6. *give a false impression*

> ● "I know that my public comments and my silence about this matter gave a false impression."
>
> —President Bill Clinton, *New York Times*, Aug. 18, 1998

One of the most chilling and terrifying uses of doublespeak occurred in 1981 when then–Secretary of State Alexander Haig was testifying before Congressional committees about the murder of three American nuns and a Catholic lay worker in El Salvador. The four women had been raped and then shot at close range, and there was clear evidence that the crime had been committed by soldiers of the Salvadoran government. Before the House Foreign Affairs Committee, Secretary Haig said:

"I'd like to suggest to you that some of the investigations would lead one to believe that perhaps the vehicle the nuns were riding in may have tried to run a roadblock or may accidentally have been perceived to have been doing so, and there'd been an exchange of fire, and then perhaps those who inflicted the casualties sought to cover it up. And this could have been at a very low level of both competence and motivation in the context of the issue itself. But the facts on this are not clear enough for anyone to draw a definitive conclusion."

The next day, before the Senate Foreign Relations Committee, Secretary Haig claimed that press reports on his previous testimony were "inaccurate." When Senator Claiborne Pell asked whether Secretary Haig was suggesting the possibility that "the nuns may have run through a roadblock," Secretary Haig replied, "You mean that they tried to violate . . . ? Not at all, no, not at all. My heavens! The dear nuns who raised me in my parochial schooling would forever isolate me from their affections and respect." When Senator Pell asked Secretary Haig, "Did you mean that the nuns were firing at the people, or what did 'an exchange of fire' mean?" Secretary Haig replied, "I haven't met any pistol-packing nuns in my day, Senator. What I meant was that if one fellow starts shooting, then the next thing you know they all panic." Thus did the Secretary of State of the United States explain official government policy on the murder of four American citizens in a foreign land.

Secretary Haig's testimony implies that the women were in some way responsible for their own fate. By using such vague wording as "would lead one to believe" and "may accidentally have been perceived to have been" he avoids any direct assertion. The use of the phrase "inflicted the casualties" not only avoids using the word "kill" but also implies that at the worst the killings were accidental or justifiable. The result of this testimony is that the Secretary of State has become an apologist for murder. This is indeed language in defense of the indefensible—language designed to make lies sound truthful and murder respectable, language designed to give an appearance of solidity to pure wind.

—*New York Times*, Mar. 29, 1981

7. *to further a version radically different from the truth*

● Oliver North testified that he "was provided with input that was radically different from the truth. I assisted in furthering that version."

—*Taking the Stand: The Testimony of Lt. Col. Oliver L. North*, Pocket Books, 1987

8. *misrepresent the facts*

● Oliver North said that "it was wrong to misrepresent the facts to Congress."

—*Taking the Stand: The Testimony of Lt. Col. Oliver L. North*, Pocket Books, 1987

9. *willful withholding of information*

● Robert McFarlane pleaded guilty to four violations of willful withholding of information from Congress. "That's a long way from lying," McFarlane said.

—*New York Times*, Mar. 15, 1988

10. *economical with the actualité*

11. *economical with the truth*

> • In England, the Defense Minister advised arms deal-
> ers who were selling arms to Iraq to be "economical
> with the actualité" when applying for export licenses.
> Later, a Foreign Office official said those involved in
> these transactions "were being economical with the
> truth" when answering questions from Parliament.
> —*Chicago Tribune*, July 21, 1993

love *n.*

1. *creative altruism*

> • "A scientific research center in creative altruism" has
> been established. Creative altruism is another term for
> love.   —*Plus*, Dec. 1987

2. *emotional concomitant*

misbehave *v.*

1. *engage in negative attention-getting*
2. *exhibit leadership charisma*

> • The mother of a two-year-old who was attending a
> play group was told that her daughter had "leadership
> charisma." It meant her daughter was bossy.
> —*Quarterly Review of Doublespeak*, Oct. 1989

3. *engage in inappropriate behavior*

pencil *n.*

portable hand-held communications inscriber (DOD)

> • According to U.S. Senator Ted Stevens, the Pentagon
> calls a pencil a "portable hand-held communications
> inscriber."   —*Phoenix Gazette*, Aug. 28, 1983

pencil sharpener *n.*
manually operated graphitic marking device acuitization
system

> • For the Canadian military, a pencil sharpener is a
> "manually operated graphitic marking device acuitiza-
> tion system.   —*Toronto Star,* Apr. 20, 1990

read *v.*
1. *interact with print*
2. *decode*

re-run *n.*
encore broadcast

road sign *n.*
ground-mounted confirmatory route markers

> • A spokesperson for the Massachusetts Department of
> Public Works, calls them "ground-mounted confirma-
> tory route markers." You probably call them road signs,
> but then you don't work in a government agency.
>   —*Boston Globe,* Apr. 4, 1988

talk (TO ONESELF) *v.*
engage in audible verbal self-reinforcement

> • A parent was dismayed when the school her son
> attends reported that he "engages in audible verbal
> self-reinforcement" until she realized that it meant he
> talks to himself.
>   —*Quarterly Review of Doublespeak,* July 1988

talk (TO SOMEONE) *v.*
1. *interface*

> • A skill very much in demand is "interfacing." Job applicants must be able to "interface" with customers, technical staff, management and probably other interfacers. Doesn't anyone just talk anymore?
> —*Quarterly Review of Doublespeak*, Oct. 1988

2. *interact*
3. *dialogue*

used videotape *n.*
1. *previously viewed video*
2. *previewed video*

videotaped *mod.*
1. *plausible live time*
2. *live on tape*

wristwatch *n.*
personal time control center

> • Among its 600 wristwatch models, Seiko Time Corporation offers 17 that have both digital displays and real hands. "We call them Personal Time Control Centers," a Seiko spokesman says.
> —*Wall Street Journal*, Jan. 1, 1983

Index of Terms and Definitions

....

Note: Terms appear in **boldface**; definitions appear in *italics*.